THE ONE-PAGE SALES COACH

Your Guide to Getting **Yes**
from Anyone, Anyplace, Anytime

DEAN MINUTO

11 REASONS WHY
You Should Read This One Book

FACT: There are 349,363* books available on "Sales"

This book distills them into <u>1 SIMPLE TOOL</u> that you and your Team can use on the back of a napkin to help you get to yes faster and more often (*see the One Page Sales Coach graphic on the next page*).

FACT: There are 65,245 books on "Influence"

This book delivers <u>7 STRATEGIES</u> (*laid out in the MAGNETS cards graphic on the next page*). Each of them taken by themselves could help you to attract more yeses, together they will help you to understand the triggers of decision making.

FACT: There are 548,151 books out there on "Marketing"

This book summarizes them in <u>3 WORDS</u> that you will use to guarantee that decision makers are listening to, and impacted personally by, your message.

These counts on 5/11/2013 from Amazon.com

1 SIMPLE TOOL

(See LESSON 2 for the One-Page Sales Coach.)

7 STRATEGIES

(See LESSON 4 for the MAGNETS.)

3 WORDS

 ALPHA DELTA VIDEŌ

(See LESSON 5 for the definitions and application.)

ABOUT THE AUTHOR

Dean Minuto helps professionals get to "yes" faster and more often from the people they are trying to influence. Dean teaches massively distilled summary courses to CEOs within the world's leading CEO membership organizations and to industry groups across the United States.

9,000 CEOs and sales executives personally trained since 1992

350 workshops on better sales messaging in the last three years

22 years of identifying sales best practices

4.9 average rating on a 5-point scale from CEOs attending Talks

1 simple guide to help you get to yes faster

Reach Dean directly at **dean@onepagesalescoach.com** with questions regarding coaching or if you'd like to have Dean deliver a Keynote (90 minutes) or Workshop (1/2 Day, One-Day or Two-Day) for your group.

---

www.OnePageSalesCoach.com

KEYNOTES

WORKSHOPS

COACHING

www.OnePageSalesCoach.com

Free tools and tips available at:
www.OnePageSalesCoach.com

This book is available at special quantity discounts to use as premiums and sales
promotions, or for use in corporate training programs. For details on bulk orders and
info on Keynotes and Workshops please go to www.OnePageSalesCoach.com

The four-box OPSC logo is a trademark of Teligent Corporation (registration pending).
One Page Sales Coach® Teligent Corporation

ISBN-10: 1475174349
ISBN-13: 9781475174342
Library of Congress Control Number: 2012906629
CreateSpace, North Charleston, SC

THE ONE-PAGE SALES COACH

Your Guide to Getting **Yes**
from Anyone, Anyplace, Anytime

DEAN MINUTO

Problems *before*	Solutions *after*
Dollars Data Delta	
Outcomes *great news* Do Done Demo 1. 2. 3.	Commitment *next steps*

CONTENTS

For Devon
Who loves you, baby?

(Always remember:
anything, anywhere, anytime.)

THE NAPKIN TEST

The CEO seated across from me at the elegant steakhouse leaned forward. He asked me the same question they always ask.

"Would it be all right if I kept *that*?"

He wanted my bar napkin, the little piece of paper I had carried over from the cocktail lounge. Actually, he wanted what was written on the napkin. On this one small napkin were all the instructions the CEO needed to get a certain person to give him a yes answer. It was, in fact, a script for him to follow.

In the last twenty-two years, I've coached more than nine thousand CEOs and sales executives in dozens of industries, and what I've found is that everyone needs a yes from someone. All I need is one sheet of paper to guide them in how to get that yes. Invariably, when the coaching session happens in a restaurant or bar, they always ask me for the napkin or placemat when we're done talking.

Let me ask you a question: *Who do you need to get a yes from?*

In the next ninety days, hearing a yes from what one person would make all the difference to you, whether personally or professionally?

I'm asking you that because this book contains **a powerful and simple tool**—the only one of its kind, because you can build it on a single sheet of paper—that will help you get that yes faster than ever.

What led up to the CEO asking for the napkin? That morning I had delivered a three-hour workshop to a group of a dozen CEOs. When I finished my talk, one of them waited for me to get done packing up my laptop and said, "Dean, I have to ask you to dinner tonight. May I take you to Morton's, and we'll get a great steak and have a drink? I need your help."

This CEO of a publicly traded bank knew he needed to get a yes from a dissident shareholder before the upcoming annual shareholder meeting. He wanted some coaching to ensure that this shareholder would support him in making the changes he wanted.

We started our conversation in the cocktail lounge. I grabbed a bar napkin and drew a vertical line down the center. Then I drew a horizontal line across the middle of the napkin, creating four boxes. I labeled the upper-left box *Problems*, the top-right box *Solutions*, the bottom-left box *Outcomes*, and the bottom-right box *Commitment*. We worked our way through the four boxes over dinner.

I asked the CEO to help me see the *problems* (box 1) from the investor's perspective—to tell me about this investor's current situation. What was the investor seeing as problems in 3D— Dollars, Data and Delta (quantifiable issues, qualitative issues, and the potential changes in his/her world that would result from solving them)?

What followed (working our way through all four boxes) is the reason the CEO was so interested in keeping the napkin.

A few weeks later, I received this note from the CEO: "Just got back from vacation to decompress from the shareholder meeting... We 'ran the table' and won all contested aspects of the election. Thanks for your help."

He had gotten the yes he needed.

And you can get the yes you need as well.

Sometimes we can create that one page in forty-five minutes; in the case of a more complex sale, it will take longer. But inevitably the person I'm coaching wants the piece of paper, because it lays out exactly the path he needs to follow to get yes faster.

In addition to the One-Page Sales Coach tool, I also will share with you *seven strategies* that you can use to attract a yes like magnets attract metals. These magnetic strategies for getting a yes are really the summation of more than one hundred years of study in what is called "the decision sciences" (behavioral psychology, et al). This book also contains *three critical words* (known since ancient times, and proven by the latest findings in science) that researchers have proven you can use to trigger a yes faster than anything you have tried before.

You are holding in your hands the summary of the key learning and best practices from my twenty years of sales coaching—and the best news is that I have delivered it in a guidebook you can read on a short plane ride. You'll find all of the above framed as six lessons that you can read in ninety minutes and apply immediately to getting your next yes faster than ever before.

The One-Page Sales Coach is your guide to getting YES from anyone, anyplace, anytime.

And if you want tools that can work for you even faster than ninety minutes then check out the ninety second summaries that are available on my website at **www.OnePageSalesCoach.com** and use them as a "check list" to prepare for your next meeting, presentation or proposal.

I am grateful for the opportunity to contribute to your continued success.

LESSON 1

MAKE A DIFFERENCE

Difference

Everybody needs a yes from someone. CEOs need to get yes from investors, VPs need to get yes from their CEOs, dentists need to get yes from patients—we all need to get a yes. Think about it. There is someone you need to hear a yes from in the coming month or quarter that would make all the difference to you. My career has been a quest to seek out and *apply knowledge* about what works in getting yes. In fact, I named my corporation Teligent because the word *intelligence* means "applied knowledge." When I named my company, my father, who spent his career at IBM, asked, "*Teligent*? What's wrong? Was *Tupid* taken?"—which just proves that if you ever feel too proud and full of yourself, just give your dad a call. Funny line, Pop.

Actually, my father, Michael Minuto, is my biggest supporter. He and my daughter Devon are the biggest inspirations in my life. About four times a week, I receive a text message from my father that reads, "Good morning. Tell Devon I love you all. MAKE A DIFFERENCE. Dad"

This is the story of my twenty-year quest to find applied sales knowledge that will *make a difference* in helping you get to the yeses that you need. My hope is that you will benefit from the wisdom I have picked up along the way from the thousands of clients I've coached.

If I could only share *one thing* with you, if you could only read up to this page, here is the key message of my work and this book:

Success in selling is not about
making a commission.

Success in selling is about
making a difference.

What's unique about this book is this: it outlines a simple and powerful tool that you can use on a single page to contribute more for your clients.

This is really what all selling is about: making a contribution. Sales isn't about getting everyone to buy the products and service you offer. Selling is about the contrast between the customer's current situation and his or her desired situation. In other words, impacting the customer's world for the better is the goal. To the degree that you make a difference, you deserve to earn a commission or you deserve to be in business. Our commission is commensurate with the difference we make.

Lessons of History

In my leisure time, I enjoy reading works of history. Maybe the most iconic work of history took husband and wife team Will and Ariel Durant forty years to complete. They started writing *The Story of Civilization* in 1935. They completed the eleven-volume set in 1975, just a few years before Will died. Forty years, eleven volumes, 9,946 pages. In the process, Will was awarded both a Pulitzer Prize and a Presidential Medal of Freedom. The Durant's created a total historical immersion, from the ancient Greeks all the way through the age of Napoleon. So, when it comes to works of history, this is the one for those of us who are interested in this stuff.

When I went online to look for *The Story of Civilization* for sale, I found a complete set in a bookstore in the Midwest. The bookseller had all eleven volumes, unopened and in perfect condition. The set was costly, but it was brand new. I ordered it, and its shipping weight was over thirty-six pounds. Each volume averages over nine hundred pages, with several of them being well over one thousand pages. No doubt about it, this is a monumental work of scholarship. These books were going to keep me busy reading for several years.

When I sent my credit card information to the bookseller, he sent me an email: "I'm just packaging up your books and I wanted to make an offer to you. Before he died, Will Durant wrote one more volume, which he considered a summary of all that he had learned. He called it *Lessons of History*. This book is just 128 pages, and with your permission, I'd like to include it in your order for an extra $10."

"Sold," I replied.

But imagine that. After writing nearly ten thousand pages, Will felt compelled to provide *a summary in 128 pages.*

This reminded me of a quotation from the scholar Blaise Pascal:

> **"I would have written a shorter**
> **letter if I had more time."**

I have taken the time to write you a shorter book. Will's desire to encapsulate his knowledge into a slender volume resonated with me. I've now spent more than twenty years seeking knowledge in sales performance. My goal is to provide the entire sum of that knowledge in a short book—a summary if you will—for business owners, executives, sales professionals, and CEOs (the number-one salesperson in any organization).

Through the years, I've distilled the best practices I've learned down to a one-page coaching tool (and a few key acronyms for easy memorization) so I can easily coach others in the approach. My hope is that every sales executive that reads this book will be able to do the same. You too can become a One-Page Sales Coach—and help your team get yes from anyone, anyplace, anytime.

Preparation is the key. Use this one-page approach to help your employees prepare for big presentations, to train salespeople for winning proposals, and to assist you in getting ready to close a big deal. My gift to you is a sheet of paper that summarizes everything I've learned in the past two decades about closing deals. Use this one page to make a difference in your customer's world.

What Do You Want to Be When You Grow Up?

I wish you could have been there the day my daughter, Devon, who is now a teenager, came home from the fourth grade and said it was career day. All the girls had been interviewed on what they wanted to be when they grew up.

This was not the first time a teacher had asked my daughter that question. Back in kindergarten Devon's answer was

> **"I want to be a nun, a painter,
> and a horsey rider."**

When she said that, I called her principal, Sister Mary Ellen, and told her "Sister, you're doing a great job!" (That's because my goal is to keep my daughter away from boys.)

But in the fourth grade, Devon had a new answer. "Devon, tell me what some of the other girls' answers were," I said.

She said Kimberly wanted to be a scientist. Well, that makes all the sense in the world; Kimberly's dad works for Lockheed Martin. Another one of the little girls, whose father is a physician, said she wanted to be a doctor. Again, a logical choice. But now my curiosity was really piqued.

"Devon, what did you tell your teacher?" I asked.

> **"Daddy,"** she held her head up high,
> **"I want to be a sales coach."**

At first I thought, Maybe I've done my daughter an injustice. She could reach higher in life. But then I realized that to be a sales coach, to teach people how to make a difference and how to improve their customer's condition, is a very honorable profession. Even a schoolgirl could see that.

(Note to Devon: Both of your answers made your father proud. No pressure, baby, I won't hold you to what you said in kindergarten or the fourth grade. Just know that both your mom and I believe you can be anything you want to be in life.)

Remember: seek not to make a commission, but always to make a difference.

OVERVIEW

You're probably wondering if you should invest the time and energy required to read this book. Well, let me ask you a few questions:

What if you could know what the top sales performers in every industry do and you could apply those practices yourself, using a simple one-page tool with four simple steps, to increase your contribution to your customers?

What if you could understand why people say yes—and turn your sales efforts into magnets for attracting more sales?

What if you could do all that in less than ninety minutes?

You can.

This book provides the answers to these questions. And, it provides easy ways (simple acronyms like **OPSC** and **MAGNETS**) to remember and to apply this knowledge so that you can make your contribution clear and get yes from any person, anyplace and anytime.

You'll learn many sales tips from this book, but there are only three laws of selling:

LAW 1: Questions control the conversation.

LAW 2: Price always matters in the absence of any other reason, and there are always other reasons.

LAW 3: Success is directly proportionate to preparation.

The One-Page Sales Coach Summary

Everyone today faces a time crunch. There always seems to be too much to do and too little time to do it. But there's always time for preparation with the One-Page Sales Coach. The full One-Page Sales Coach approach is covered in detail in the next lessons. Here is a quick overview.

Take out a pen and a blank sheet of paper. Draw a line down the center of the page and a line across the middle—two lines to divide the page into four boxes. Label the four boxes Problems (before), Solutions (after), Outcomes (great news), and Commitment (next steps). Draw a triangle (the universal mathematical symbol for delta, meaning *change* or *difference*) between box 1 and box 2. It should look like this:

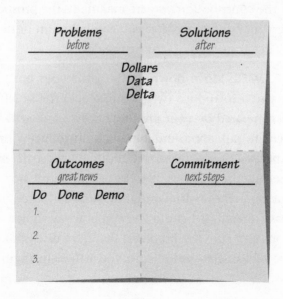

Prepare for your presentation with any target (client, prospect, your boss—anyone you want a yes from) by using the following steps.

1. PROBLEMS. Start with the *before* box to understand where that person is right now. Ask questions to uncover the target's current situation. Find out what the prospect person has tried before and what is preventing him or her from getting what she wants. Focus on seeing clearly that person's current condition in 3D: DOLLARS, DATA and DELTA—(quantifiable measures, important business areas the potential change in these areas that impact the prospect directly).

2. SOLUTIONS. Proceed to the *after* box of the grid. Ask questions to understand the target's goals, wants, and desires. What will his or her world look like *after* working with you? What goes up or down—what changes in your prospect's world in the three main areas: Dollars, Data and Delta? (The bigger the difference between *problem* and *solution*, the bigger the contribution you are making to the prospect, the greater your confidence that you can help him or her—and the greater your odds of closing the deal.)

3. OUTCOMES. Move down to the *great news* box. This is where you'll introduce (with confidence) the specific outcomes generated by your product or service. You've earned the right to talk about outcomes—to introduce a prescription—because you've taken the time to diagnose the *problems* and identify the *solutions*. You can ask for permission to outline the outcomes with a question, such as "Based on what you have shared, if I could show you a way to achieve the solutions and cure the problems you have discussed, would that be of value to you?" And you will help them to see those outcomes in 3D: DO, DONE and DEMO (share what you Do, who you have Done it for, and provide a Demonstration for them).

4. COMMITMENT. A presentation ends by proceeding to the *next steps* box. This is when you summarize and gain a clear commitment for the next step in the process. What are the next steps you both agree to take to begin the process and achieve the solutions, to cure the problems?

On to the Four Boxes

In the next lesson, we'll take a closer look at **problems, solutions, outcomes,** and **commitment**, or OPSC (which also stands for One-Page Sales Coach). This acronym is easy to remember, so you can use it every time.

These are the four basics to sales success, and the four boxes will guide you as you prepare for any presentation. They are the key to the One-Page Sales Coach method.

KEY QUESTION

ARE YOU MAKING A DIFFERENCE?

PERSONAL ACTION SUMMARY

Make a list of action items taken from your reading of this book:

_____

_____

_____

_____

_____

_____

_____

_____

_____

_____

_____

_____

_____

_____

_____

_____

_____

_____

_____

_____

_____

_____

_____

_____

_____

_____

LESSON 2

MAKE IT SIMPLE

Simple

*In this lesson, I'll discuss the four basic steps consistent with every consultative sales model and provide you the simple acronym OPSC to remember them. We can only talk about **outcomes** and ask for **commitments** after we have identified the **solutions** to our client's **problems**.*

In 1990, As far as I knew at the time, I was the only consultant hired directly out of college for a consulting group within The Dun & Bradstreet Corporation (familiar to most business people as D&B, the credit report firm). Our goal was to help other businesses generate sales results using D&B's data. The number-one salesperson in that group at the time was a guy who has become a dear friend and a mentor to me, Steve Rand.

Just out of college, I was fearless getting in front of prospects, but I didn't know how to sell the D&B data and information.

So the first path I was directed to follow was to learn about

THE ONE-PAGE SALES COACH

becoming a "closer." I read all the books I could find about closing sales and listened to the ra-rah stuff from some amazing old-school sales trainers like J. Douglas Edwards, Tom Hopkins, and Zig Ziglar.

I learned more than a dozen closes: the puppy-dog close (take it home and try it), the alternate of choice (this or that), and the Ben Franklin balance sheet (let's do what smart Old Ben used to do). And then there was the Columbo close: ask one question before leaving. Remember the Peter Falk character in the rumpled raincoat that used to do this in those TV detective stories? Lt. Columbo would always start to leave so the suspect would let his guard down, and then he would turn around and say, "I have one more question." According to the books I was told to read and the recordings I was told to listen to, these closes worked every time. (Experience later proved that they really DON'T work.)

Salespeople who grew up in that world remember those closes. So I was really, really fired up to learn how the top sales rep at D&B (my mentor, Steve) closed business. I invited him to lunch and asked, "Steve, tell me the secret. How do *you* close? What's the close you use?"

Steve laughed, pushed himself away from the table, and grandly said, "Close? I don't close!"

"What are you talking about?" I asked. "Everyone's telling me that sales is about being a closer. How do you close?"

"Dino, let me make this clear," he replied. "I invest a lot of time diagnosing my customer's needs, understanding their world, and then coming up with a solution that meets their needs in a way they never thought of. You know what? If after spending all that time they don't say yes, then they're too stupid to be my customer."

That was a tremendous insight. It was about making a difference and knowing that Steve wasn't selling a product. What he was doing was changing their world, and doing so confidently.

His goal was to make a difference for his clients.

Steve used to travel out to Los Angeles often. He'd sit out by the hotel pool, and there would be people in the movie business all around him. I refer to Steve as the Jewish James Bond: he's very handsome and is always elegantly dressed. When he wears a suit, it is a hand-tailored Italian suit made from expensive fabric. Plus, he is very well spoken. Steve always knows just the right words to say, like those characters in a movie that come up with the most amazing lines.

People in Los Angeles would ask Steve what he did for a living, and he decided he had to come up with a different answer than "I sell data."

"So, Dino," he told me, "what I tell them is *I'm in the hopes and dreams business*. That may sound corny, but that's really what I do. I find out what my customers want to achieve, not just for their businesses but in their personal lives. And everything I do is about helping them get there."

True confession time. I didn't believe that was all Steve did. So I would wait until everyone went home, then find my way into his file cabinet and take his proposals out to photocopy them—because I was convinced there had to be a secret. What was he doing different that made him number one?

By studying his proposals, I learned how he started with the customer's background and *problems*, before ever getting into talking about anything about Dun & Bradstreet. I saw the amount of time he took to understand the client's world and how it could be improved by quantifying *solutions*, and then to outline specific *outcomes* with next steps and time-lines for a *commitment*. I began to understand.

Have You Worked at McDonald's Yet?

Years later, I left Dun & Bradstreet, moved to the West Coast, and started my own consulting business. I had brought on several clients, and everything was going so well. But then an act of God happened: the Northridge earthquake. My wife and I decided that California was a bit "unstable" (a week of aftershocks will convince you of that), and we moved back to Philadelphia, where her family lived. I restarted my business there.

You know what? Philadelphia is a tough town, the only town I've know where sports fans throw snowballs at Santa. I spent months trying to bring on clients—working every day, making calls, having appointments—but I wasn't closing any business. I really started to question whether I had lost whatever sales magic I had learned. Fear, uncertainty, and doubt had crept into my head. (I now know that this is a common event among salespeople.) It was devastating.

Sometimes a line from an old movie says it all. At that time, for me it was a Donald Sutherland film called *Citizen X* and the line

> **"If you spend enough time with a lion, the idea of roaring starts to become more and more reasonable."**

I decided to go back to the lions that I knew to figure out what they were doing. This is part of the secret of success. If you want to roar like a lion, start hanging out with them.

So I called the biggest sales lion I knew and said, "Hello, Steve, its Dean."

"Hello, Dino!" he exclaimed.

I paused. "Steve, I need your help."

"Well, I'm honored that you called."

"Steve, I think I've forgotten how to sell."

He started laughing. "This is ridiculous. What do you mean?" I told him what had been going on: I'm there in Philly, I wasn't closing, and could he help me.

"Dino, *please*. You've always been successful at selling. You've always known how to close deals. You learned when you were at Dun & Bradstreet, and then you went off on your own. Think about last year, all those deals you closed. So here's the thing—what were you doing last year? You need to get back to doing that."

I said, "Steve, I don't remember. That's why I'm calling you."

He laughed again. "Okay, I've just read an article about working at McDonald's and the percentage of young people who have worked at McDonald's. It's this amazing incredibly high percentage of American males in your age category Dean, between fifteen and thirty. You're in that age category, right?"

I said yes. (I was twenty-five at the time.)

"Well, this huge percentage of people in your age category have worked at McDonald's. Have you worked at McDonald's yet?"

I said no.

He paused and said, "Well, you still have *that* to look forward to, don't you?"

And he hung up the phone.

The Four Basics as Four Boxes

It felt like Steve had stuck a knife in my chest. When I tell this story to salespeople, they laugh hysterically. Imagine a guy you admire, a guy you look up to, a guy you idolize when it comes to selling, and you call and ask him for help, and he says, "Time for you to go work at McDonald's." At least, that's what I thought he said.

But, like I said, for Steve, life is like someone already wrote the script for him. Often I walk away and then I realize what he was saying. Talking to him is like getting a paper cut and you don't even realize you're bleeding until you are ten paces away and you've bled all over your sleeve.

So the next day I realized what he was saying: selling is simple, but we can complicate it. There are basics. You know what the basics are, and you need to get back to the basics.

The basic ingredients for success in selling for me and everyone I have studied, are as follows:

1. Probe and uncover pains and *problems*.

2. Clearly define (and quantify) the *solutions*.

3. Only then introduce the *outcomes* of working with you (with confidence).

4. Mutually agree what's happening next by getting a *commitment*.

Problems. Solutions.
Outcomes. Commitment.

Those are the four basics of selling and the four boxes of the One-Page Sales Coach approach. The next section illustrates how to use these four boxes to improve each step of your sales process and your sales results.

THE ONE-PAGE
SALES COACH

Everything I've learned about selling in the last twenty years, I'm going to distill into one page for you right now. If a CEO asked me to coach him before he went in front of a shareholder meeting, this is what I would say. If a sales rep wanted me to coach her before a major presentation, this is how I would advise her. If I sat next to a representative in a call center, same thing. And I've used this tool thousands of times over the years to help people get to yes faster.

In any scenario, I would ask them to take out a pen and a piece of paper, and I have them draw exactly what I'm going to have you draw right now.

Here is your lesson on how to be a One-Page Sales Coach. Take out a sheet of paper. When you're the trainer, have the person or the people you are coaching do the same.

Draw a line down the center of your page from the top to the bottom.

The Top Two Boxes—Diagnosis

On the top of the left side, write the word *Problems* and below that the word *before*.

On the top of the right side, write the word *Solutions* and below that the word *after*. Draw a triangle (the symbol for "difference") on the middle line, separating the two boxes

On the left side of the page, describe your target's world right now. What are the *problems* in that world? Describe that world and what's going on in it. What's the current situation? What's the pain in that prospect's world without you?

On the right side of the page, describe what the prospect wants, or what you know would change his or her situation. What would make his or her world better after you help? This is a word picture of a better future.

Three ways to categorize a prospect's *problems* and *solutions* are Dollars, Data and Delta. Try and "see them clearly" in 3D (Dollars, Data, and Delta). These are the quantitative and qualitative areas that you can change in his/her world. These can be written in the before and after boxes of the grid.

Your sheet of paper should look like this:

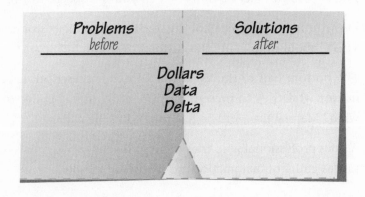

DOLLARS. Can you describe in dollars and cents what's going on in your target's world? Are there specific monetary metrics you can measure? What would a better dollar situation look like?

DATA. Are there processes you can improve? What would a better process look like—and can you document that improvement with data?

DELTA. What's going to change in your prospect's world? How is this affecting him or her on an individual level? What would an improved situation look like—both to them within their organization and out of the organization?

For each *problem* that you list on the left, what goes up or down in your customer's world as a result of you *solving* it? These two boxes should help you understand what's happening in the prospect's world and how your offer could change that for the better. Do not proceed until you have a clear picture of the *before and after (the Delta)*. Have a clear picture of how you can make a difference in your prospect's world.

Everything in the top half of the sheet is about the customer. This is about diagnosing the customer's world.

The bottom half of the sheet is about your prescription. A doctor who tries to prescribe before diagnosis is guilty of what? Malpractice. And he just might kill the patient.

A sales professional who tries to prescribe before diagnosis is just as guilty of malpractice and might kill the deal.

Turn Two Boxes into Four—
Move from Diagnosis to Prescription

Now draw a line across the center of the page from left border to right border, turning the one sheet into a four-box grid.

On the top of the lower-left side box, write the word *Outcomes* and below that the words *great news*.

On the top of the lower-right side box, write the word *Commitment* and below that the words *next steps*.

Your sheet of paper should look like this:

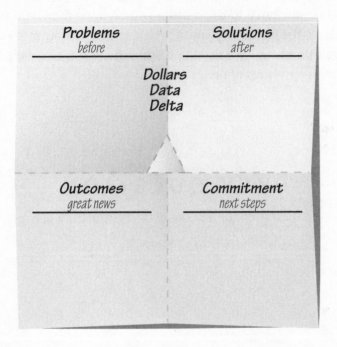

Now, it's important that we talk about your investment of time completing the top two boxes—more importantly the Return on Investment, which will be the marked increase in your level of confidence these two boxes will generate—and not only your confidence, but also the effect your confidence will have on the confidence of your target (the person you want a yes from). Some have referred to this as a *secret effect* (actually the basis of the book *The Secret* that caused a stir a few years ago).

The so-called secret, which really is no secret, is this: ***Selling is a transfer of emotion***—a transfer of belief—between you and your customer.

Remember the top two boxes are all about *diagnosis*, and before we move to the bottom two boxes—where you will discuss the *prescription* you are offering your customer to cure their problems—we need to discuss the power of beliefs on the effectiveness of prescriptions.

KEY QUESTION

ARE YOU MAKING A DIFFERENCE?

PERSONAL ACTION SUMMARY

Make a list of action items taken from your reading of this book:

LESSON 3

MAKE IT BELIEVABLE

Believable

In this lesson, we'll discuss the power of expectancy theory and how our confident belief in outcomes makes those outcomes more likely.

My wish is that the One-Page Sales Coach approach will make a believer out of you. I believe your sales effort will be more successful because of it.

Belief is powerful medicine—not just figuratively, but also literally. There are cases chronicled monthly in places as varied as *Scientific American* magazine and the *Wall Street Journal* outlining what's known as "the placebo effect." When patients (and physicians) are confident in the effectiveness of a prescription (even if it is a placebo and not the medicine), there is a marked decrease in their perception of pain and an increase in the speed of their healing. (See the February 2009 *Scientific American* as well as "Why Placebos Work Wonders" from the January 3, 2012, issue of the *Wall Street Journal*.)

Belief makes the difference for many patients in the outcomes of their treatments. In recent decades, reports have confirmed the efficacy of various placebo treatments—substances containing no medication and prescribed or given to reinforce a patient's expectation to get well—in nearly all areas of medicine. Placebos have helped alleviate pain, depression, anxiety, and even inflammatory disorders. I'm not suggesting that all doctors believe in the placebo effect—in fact many of them absolutely do not—but the effect has been documented.

The placebo effect is based on the science of expectancy theory, which proposes that a person decides to behave or act in a certain way because of what she *expects* the result of that selected behavior will be. Expectancy theory, first proposed by professors such as Victor Vroom of the Yale School of Management, is about the mental processes regarding choice. The theory explains how choices are made and decisions are effected by **beliefs in outcomes**.

Belief makes it real not only in medicine but also in the movies and in sales. This chapter is about the effect that using the One-Page Sales Coach approach has on *your* confidence as well as on the confidence, or belief, of the person you are presenting to on the other side of the table.

Let's start by thinking about what the word *expectation* means.

When we expect something to happen, we have an *internal belief* that it's going to happen. The more we expect it to happen, the more likely it will be to happen. This is where the term "self-fulfilling prophesy" comes from. In effect, belief makes it real in many cases.

There's another interesting aspect of the placebo effect: it effects not only the patient but their doctor. You can read the articles mentioned above for more data, but the bottom line is that when a doctor really believes that the treatment she's prescribing will help that patient, the patient's belief increases as well. The patient is then more confident in the medicine, and that increases the likelihood of the success of the treatment. But when a doctor doesn't believe that a medicine will help a patient, it tends not to help. Patients pick up expectation cues from doctors. And your prospects pick up expectation cues from you.

While this is a modern area of study, it's actually really ancient as well. Basically, every book of wisdom (the output of Philosophers and religious writers throughout history), definitely including the Old and New Testaments in the **Bible** (from one thousand years ago), contains passages like "To those who believe, even more shall be given." At the end of the nineteenth century, James Allen said in his beautiful book **As a Man Thinketh**, "As a man thinketh, so is he."

In other words, thoughts are real things. They leave a mark, if you will. Our thoughts mark us just as much as a dog bite could leave a mark. If you put pressure with one hand on the wrist of your other hand, when you take your hand away, you see that you've left a mark. Thoughts and expectations leave a mark too. *Some thoughts not only mark us, they make us.*

Our thoughts and beliefs leave a mark on us, but also on the person receiving a presentation from us. This is what happens: the more we know by doing our diagnosis and learning about the customer's situation and the potential improvements she can make, the greater our belief that we can making an impact and help her. Naturally, that increases our confidence.

When you are more confident, the prospect can sense it. Professional salespeople have known for more than half a century that the person on the other side of the message is influenced positively by the salesperson's belief in what he is selling. Your prospect absolutely feels it, just as you have felt when you have dealt with a salesperson who was convinced in the worth of his product or service, or just as you believe your doctor when she is absolutely confident in the prescription she has given you.

Emotions, such as feelings of belief, can be felt and transferred. Personally, I find this fascinating, whether it's a doctor transferring his belief in a prescription or a sales professional transferring his belief in a sales proposal. Price Pritchett, in his book **Hard Optimism**, documented the fact that optimism is the difference maker for people who live longer and people who are highly successful.

Optimism can be contagious. Fifty years ago, there was a famous sales trainer and author by the name of J. Douglas Edwards, hailed as the father of the modern sales approach, who defined selling: "Selling is a transfer of emotions." In other words *when you believe* and feel confident in something, then *the customer is more likely to believe it* and feel it also.

How confident are you that you will make a difference in the world of the person you want that yes from? The One-Page Sales Coach approach provides the means for you to increase your confidence and thereby increase your prospect's confidence.

Let's return to the analogy of medicine: what must a doctor do before writing a prescription? She has to diagnose the patient, which is analogous to the probing of a customer's *problems*, and also identify how much *solutions* could change the patient's world. The top two quadrants of the One-Page Sales Coach tool, **Problems** and **Solutions**, are about diagnosis. The two bottom quadrants, **Outcomes** and **Commitment**, are about the prescription. A doctor can prescribe medication because he first takes the time to understand your condition and then gives written instructions on how to relieve the *problem* and treat the ailment.

This book began with stories of CEOs and the One-Page Sales Coach tool being sketched out on a napkin. One of the reasons CEOs want the napkin when I get done drawing on it is that **they believe in it** as a prescription, or in short, as a script. Doctors refer to prescriptions as scripts.

Think about the word *script*. There's another profession that uses scripts, and that's acting. The key to great actors, from Meryl Streep and Angelina Jolie to Johnny Depp and Leonardo DiCaprio, is not that they were just lucky enough to get great scripts. Why these folks get paid twenty million dollars per movie to deliver the words is the belief and conviction they bring to the part. That confidence is transferred to the audience, and we are eager to see them again and again, using a variety of scripts.

Using the One-Page Sales Coach as a script is about your approach and about your delivery. What really makes the difference between an Academy Award-winning actor and someone at the local playhouse is not the script, but his style and the emotions he transfers to us. For a salesperson, the One-Page Sales Coach tool is the script, but the way you deliver it is all about your style.

Every salesperson has his or her own style. What a really good sales coach knows is to never try to coach someone on style. Be yourself (everyone else is already taken, as the saying goes) when you are in front of the person or audience you want to convince. And remember that your emotion and your belief about what you're proposing will be felt by the client. Let your One-Page Sales Coach be your script and your guide to be the best you that you can be.

A final word about how to build confidence in your delivery: *practice*. The more you prepare and practice, the more likely you'll be to have that confidence. Your confidence will increase as you invest more time preparing the One-Page Sales Coach script, thinking about your delivery, and practicing your presentation. Remember, there's a direct correlation between your level of confidence in your presentation and the level of confidence of the person listening to your presentation. Expectancy theory assures that your belief makes it real.

The Lower Two Boxes—Prescriptions

Now look at the box in the lower-left quadrant, the one labeled **Outcomes**. The **Outcomes** box is where you describe your prescription, with confidence (*great news*) for solving your prospect's problems. This box is where you should determine what you want your prospect to see clearly about your product or service—and to see in 3D here means DO, DONE AND DEMO. You want to customize a description of what you Do, who you have Done it for, and a relevant

Demo for the prospect that will most powerfully convey the outcome of working with you. And the box on the lower-right quadrant, the one labeled *Commitment*, is where you and the prospect mutually agree on what each of your *next steps* will be.

Here's how to formulate the most powerful way to describe the *Outcomes* that you want to discuss in your presentation. Look at the upper-right quadrant, the *Solutions (after)* box, and order the solutions. Which is the biggest Delta (in Dollars or Data) that the prospect can achieve? Then determine the second, the third, and so on.

Pick the *Solution* that your prospect stands to receive the most benefit from, and make that your number-one listed outcome in the lower-left box, *Outcomes (great news)*. Identify who you have done that for already (a previous client much like this one). And then find a way to demonstrate (potentially with client testimonials, or ratings, etc.) that outcome. Then make the second-biggest *Solution* your number-two item in the outcome section, and the third biggest your number-three. List only three outcomes. You do not want to overwhelm a prospect with them.

For each outcome help the person you are trying to influence to see it in 3D—tell them what you will Do, who you have Done it for, and give them a Demo.

In the lower-left box you should make those 3D's into three columns as shown in the next graphic: Do, Done and Demo.

Finally, label the lower-right box *Commitment* and below that the words *next steps*. What's the commitment you are looking for, the next steps needed?

In the **Commitment** box, make a list of what the prospect and you will do together to get started. For example, what are the appointments that need to be scheduled, the introductions to be made, the documents that need to be signed—and what is a date for each?

Now your page should look like this:

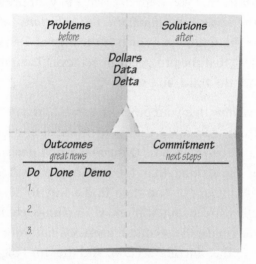

The key is to demonstrate a massive difference in the customer's world from before to after. The bigger the difference, the easier it is for prospects to know why they should use you. The smaller the difference, the more they're going to focus on price.

There's nothing new about this concept. How to show contrast was one of the lessons I've learned by reading David Ogilvy, whom *Time* magazine called "the most sought-after wizard in the advertising business." Ogilvy, who lived from 1911 to 1999, made it a mission to codify what works in persuasive communications.

In his funny and insightful books *Confessions of an Advertising Man* and *Ogilvy on Advertising*, he taught timeless lessons. One of the things Ogilvy said is, "If I'm selling fire extinguishers, I never talk about fire extinguishers in the beginning of the process. What I endeavor to do is light a fire under everyone's chair. When the room gets hot enough, I'll present a fire extinguisher as an option for them to consider."

In other words, recreate the pain (problem) in your customers' world so that they feel how the world will improve without that pain (solution).

An Example: How Vistage Solves CEO Problems

To see the concept in action, check out the Vistage International website at www.vistage.com. One of the first messages visitors to that website see is this:

VISTAGE HELPS CEOS:

BECOME BETTER LEADERS

MAKE BETTER DECISIONS

ACHIEVE BETTER RESULTS

Better leaders. Better decisions. Better results. (Those are the three outcomes that Vistage is conveying.) With more than fifteen thousand members, Vistage (once known as The Executive Committee, or TEC) is the world's foremost chief-executive leadership organization. Vistage provides members with monthly peer workshops, one-on-one business coaching, speaker presentations from hundreds of top industry experts, social networking, and an extensive online library of articles, best practices, pod-casts, and webinars.

Today Vistage and its global affiliates operate in sixteen countries. CEO members meet in small groups every month under the same guiding principles: to help one another make better decisions, achieve better results, and enhance their lives. In these groups, member CEOs learn to challenge each other with respect and caring as they interact on a wide array of topics and issues. There is a process that members and group "Chairs" follow, and that process translates into specific outcomes for members that make a difference in their lives and in their businesses.

On the Vistage website, you see those three outcomes—Better Leaders, Better Decisions, Better Results— and examples of what it is that Chairs do, who they have done it for, and demonstrations of the results.

Think about what the critical problems are for CEOs and how solutions to those problems that achieve these specific outcomes convey a better world.

BETTER LEADERS. One of the key problems for CEOs is "I'm so *in* my business, I can't work *on* my business." So the first outcome says, "We're the world's leading CEO membership organization, and we'll make you a Better Leader."

Vistage then goes about demonstrating that outcome on the website. Part of the demo is that they have other Vistage members in video testimonials talking about how their leadership skills have improved as a result of them getting out of their business and having world-class speakers come in every month.

BETTER DECISIONS. As a second problem, CEOs might say, "I'm alone. I've got no one in my personal or professional life that I trust to help me think through some really tough issues." Vistage says, "You will make Better Decisions."

What's the demo? Better decisions are the result of having a peer group of other CEOs you can bounce things off of every month, who have no goal other than to help you get better. And Vistage shows you more video testimonials and case studies from members who discuss the "Better Decisions" they've made with the support of their group.

BETTER RESULTS. The third problem involves business performance. The outcome is that you will achieve better results after you become a member than you did before you were a member. Here's the demo: by most major measures (Vistage shares the data on the website), the average Vistage member grows her business faster than the industry average after becoming a member than she did before becoming a member.

From the "before" *problems* came the "after" *solutions* and hence the *outcomes* of "Better Leaders, Better Decisions and Better Results." What Vistage has also subtly done is built an acronym from the first letter of the words *leader*, *decisions*, and *results*: LDR. What could this stand for?

LDR = LeaDeR

Simply, that's what Vistage does. It provides leadership training that helps CEOs become better leaders.

Why would Vistage want to come up with an acronym? More important, why would *you* want to come up with an acronym to describe the outcomes of working with you? The answer is, to make them easy to remember and repeat—not only for the prospects, but for you and your salespeople.

The name One-Page Sales Coach is also a memory device. The four letters of OPSC are a trigger to remember the four boxes: Outcomes, Problems, Solutions, and Commitment.

When I conduct training sessions, sometimes I have ten individuals from one company. When I ask them to describe their businesses in simple terms, guess how many answers I get? I get eleven, because one guy answers it twice because he didn't like his first answer.

Think of how much energy a company forces its sales team to use every time people ask them the question "What does your company do?" Think of what a benefit it would be to have everyone in the company consistently say what the organization is all about.

Investing the time and energy to come up with an acronym to describe what your company does can make it easier for everyone, both inside and outside your organization to know what you stand for.

For example, the three outcomes for my sales training are summed up in the three words *Accelerate*, *Close*, and *Trigger*, which together form the acronym ACT. When I'm asked what I do, the first thing that comes to my mind is that acronym, and I describe my offerings simply: "My goal is to help you get to yes faster: to help you *accelerate* your sales cycles, to *close* more business, and to *trigger* faster decisions from your clients in an honest and ethical way." The acronym ACT helps me remember and present this in a consistent way.

Consistency in what a company "stands for" can be worth a great deal. Consistency in "messaging" increases value in the case of firms large and small. Quick, what does Volvo stand for? *Safety.* They own that word in the automobile industry. That's why a Chinese company was willing to pay $1.8 billion for Volvo a few years ago. What the acquiring firm was buying was more than just a company; it was a brand that stands for something in people's minds. Volvo means safety.

What do you stand for in your customer or prospective customer's mind? Can you come up with an acronym to make that easy for everyone to remember?

Vistage One-Page Sales Coach Example

To illustrate by example, here is what a simple version of a One-Page Sales Coach sheet might look like for Vistage. This is not a sales and marketing tool that's shown to a prospect (although it certainly could be). This is a sales and marketing tool used to refine messages in marketing materials like websites and in sales presentations to prospects.

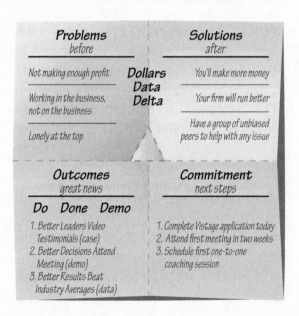

A Chinese proverb says that life is simple, but we insist on making it complicated. And many people insist on making sales complicated. This simple approach is consistent with every consultative sales model in existence. You can do it in a short time before you or one of your reps goes on a sales call.

I'm not a big believer in white, three-ring training binders explaining complex sales processes, unless you have the content memorized and are using it. I also don't believe in certificates of accomplishment from a sales training course, unless we remember something and can apply it.

Keep it simple. Keep it to one page. Make it easy to see by making it 3D: when looking at the problems show the Dollars, Data and Delta; when looking at the outcomes show the Do, Done and Demo. Show them in a way that both you and the customer believe. In a complicated world, simplicity and confidence wins out.

Not every prospect will say yes to you. But is there a way to improve your chances? Is there a way to make your presentations attract a yes as if you were using magnets? Most definitely, and those "magnets" are discussed in the next lesson. (And yes, "magnets" is an acronym for seven strategies to help you attract more yeses!)

KEY QUESTION

DO YOU BELIEVE THE OUTCOMES?

PERSONAL ACTION SUMMARY

Make a list of action items taken from your reading of this book:

_____

_____

_____

_____

_____

_____

_____

_____

_____

_____

_____

_____

_____

_____

_____

_____

_____

_____

_____

_____

LESSON 4

MAKE IT ATTRACTIVE

Attractive

In this lesson, I'll share seven strategies that attract a yes like magnets. These magnetic strategies for getting yes are a simple summation taken from studies conducted by social scientists over the last one hundred years in the area of behavioral psychology.

This is not a book on behavioral psychology—or any of the other "decision sciences". There are dozens and dozens of great books out there on those topics—and more published every month. If I were to recommend one of them, the book to read if you could only read one book in behavioral psychology as it applies to decision making is *Influence* by Dr. Robert Cialdini.

Most people don't have the time to spend reading entire books of that scale.

So in this lesson, I'll describe how I was personally influenced by Dr. Cialdini, and some of the other books on the topic of "making faster decisions" (like *Nudge* by Thaler and Sunstein, and both *The Tipping Point* and *Blink*, by Malcolm Gladwell) and more importantly, I'll give you a simple acronym, MAGNETS, which you can use to apply some of the best practices from my work for yourself.

For context, I have to go back to when I was twenty years old and just hired by Dun & Bradstreet. My first territory was the state of Connecticut.

There were many high-profile companies like GE who were D&B's clients at the time. My job was to go inside those companies and help them use Dun & Bradstreet's data, whether it was for marketing or analysis. (The more these clients sold, and the better they understood their data, the more data they would want to buy from D&B.)

At every business I visited, I noted the same thing: there were two salespeople sitting right next to each other, and one guy was selling twice as much as the other. (Have you ever seen this phenomenon? Two people in the *same job*, and one person doing *significantly better* than the other?)

If your job was to help companies sell more, and every place you went you saw one salesperson out-performing the others, what question you would ask? Naturally, you'd want to know what the more successful person was doing that the less successful person was not. Simply put, what is the difference? It's the question I asked for the next ten years at every business I visited: *What do the top performers do?* It's not rocket science. At least back then it wasn't rocket science.

Take two salespeople: Tim and John. Tim sells twice as much a month as John. Why? What does Tim do (**or *not* do**) differently to generate twice as much business as John? What I found was there were many specific actions that top-performing salespeople took. From my research, I created a database of best sales practices. Every place I went, I set out to find the top performer and what made him or her different.

What was interesting to me is this is not where most companies focus when they want to increase sales performance. They do not ask, "What are the Top Performers doing?" They ask, *"Why does everyone else suck?"*

That didn't strike me as a particularly creative question. It's easy to make a list of the ways people underperform. I made it my goal to study what the high performers were doing.

In addition to in-depth study of what top performers do, I went through every sales training course and book available to me. These included Mack Hanan's *Consultative Selling*, *SPIN Selling* by Neil Rackham, and *The New Solutions Selling* by Keith Eades, which all provide a powerful process and their own set of tools.

What I learned from studying certain top performers and the various sales processes is this: If you *do* certain things, you will *get* certain results. Any person who has been selling for any length of time learns this truth. When you follow prescribed steps, prescribed outcomes happen. The right activities lead to the right outcomes.

As I continued building this database of best sales practices, clients began asking me for access to it. Eventually I decided to focus on building a sales-training and consulting practice on my own. Glendale Federal Bank was one of my first major clients, and then my partner and I brought on GE and The Hartford. We worked with many of their call centers around the country. I then brought on Sears as a client, followed by H&R Block, and the business was off and running.

Ten years into it, I was introduced to a behavioral psychologist. One of my clients, a company called Advanta in Philadelphia, had brought in this "famous" psychologist to work with their senior executives.

I laughed to myself and said (sarcastically, if you must know the truth), "That's just the thing they need, a psychologist. That's great."

The problem was, the CEO at Advanta then said to the executives in charge of his sales teams (my clients), "You're going to start applying behavioral psychology to our sales processes."

Let's not do that, I thought. I just spent ten years focused on sales as a process. Let's not muddy the water with psychology.

Boy, was I wrong.

The PhD he brought in was Robert B. Cialdini. In the field of influence and persuasion, Dr. Cialdini is one of the most cited living psychologists in the world today. When we met he held appointments at Arizona State University as Regents' Professor of Psychology, and he also has had visiting scholar appointments at USC, UC Berkeley, and the Graduate School of Business at Stanford University.

A few paragraphs ago, I recommended to you his best-selling book, *Influence: The Psychology of Persuasion*, and if you are a "reader" like me then it is a must read if you would like to begin explaining why some salespeople are remarkably persuasive. It's the seminal work in the area of behavioral psychology as applied to sales.

I read it six times the first year. And not because I am "slow", (ok, some folks would argue that point) but because there is just so much there in terms of research and examples—and because I did not "get it" on the first read.

On the first read I was under the impression that the author (like most people) thought that all sales professionals were like con artists. But after digesting the research I understood that what was really being pointed out was that there are "triggers" that people use to make faster decisions, and certainly those triggers can be used by con artists. But they can also be used to help people make appropriate decisions faster—they can be used in an honest and non-manipulative way.

Let me give you an example of the same trigger used two different ways. Research suggests that deadlines can motivate people to make faster decisions. Example 1, a car dealer sets a deadline on your decision by saying, "Look, here's the monthly payment and this is a great deal, but my manager says this offer is only good if we hear from you by lunchtime today". And some customers would feel that deadline is manipulative, it might turn many potential customers off if they feel that the deadline was completely arbitrary. Example 2, the IRS sets a deadline of April 15 to file your personal tax return—and millions of Americans go to the post office (and stand in line) to pay their taxes on that day.

While we as taxpayers might not always appreciate paying our taxes, if we are interested in helping people to get something done then we might want to think about the best practice employed by setting a deadline which gets millions of people to do something they don't want to do. The IRS uses a real deadline—with real penalties if the deadline is not met—and it triggers people to take action.

The books I have mentioned above can help explain the psychological secrets that can trigger powerful impulses to "move" and how to use these tactics skilfully (and ethically).

When we met at Advanta, Dr. Cialdini blew me away. Because he was able to help me shine a light into the dark corners of why people make the decisions they make. And I realized that even more important than asking what the top performers do, there's a second question I should have asked: *Why do people say yes?*

The human mind is focused to save energy, and because we are bombarded with messages every day in a modern world the mind likes shortcuts when making decisions. Let's say you and a friend both live in Pennsylvania, and you decide it's time for a little roadtrip vacation. So you get your families in two cars, and you take a ride down to Florida. Now imagine your two-family caravan pulls off the road about halfway to Florida, because you're hungry. You're in a town you've never been in, and there are two diners. One diner has a parking lot *full of cars*. The other diner's lot is *completely empty*. Which diner are you attracted to? Which diner do you assume has the better food?

Naturally, you are attracted to the diner with all the cars.

That's a prime example of using a trigger—a shortcut to making a faster decision. When you pull off that road and you're in a town you've never been in, your brain doesn't want to use a ton of energy. So it looks for certain triggers. The one you just used when you said "a parking lot full of cars," is one of the most important in behavioral psychology.

The principle that psychologists call social proof states that one shortcut we use to determine what's correct is to find out what other people think is correct. As a rule, we make fewer mistakes by acting in accord with social evidence than contrary to it. This is why commercials use man-in-the street testimonial interviews.

Social proof is persuasive because we all suffer from information overload. Research evidence suggests that the ever-accelerating pace and informational crush of modern life will make automated decision making more and more prevalent. In dealing with a complicated world, we need shortcuts it is as simple as that.

When human beings are in situations of uncertainty, they look for proof of what a lot of others like them have already chosen. One of the clues you look for is proof that a lot of people like you have already chosen. You see that proof in the numbers.

Here's what we know now from additional science about that little triggering decision: It's not that you *pick* the diner that has more people, it's that you *avoid* the diner that's empty.

Let me put this to you a different way: **People don't choose the best. They avoid the risky.** And other people's safety convinces.

How to Attract Clients using MAGNETS

I went on to work with clients and to set up a certification program for training people in this research and its application to decision making. Along the way, I learned a great deal from the scientific research about why people say yes. To help salespeople easily learn and remember the principles of behavioral psychology, I put together a model for myself with seven letters in the form of an acronym—MAGNETS—to describe the main principles in behavioral psychology. On the following pages we will review what each of the letters stands for and some quick examples.

These are Seven Strategies. As laid out in the graphic on the next page and each of these strategies is a card you can play to attract a faster yes. Each one of them taken by themselves could help you to win, and taken all together they will help you to understand some of the triggers as to why people take the actions and make the decisions they make.

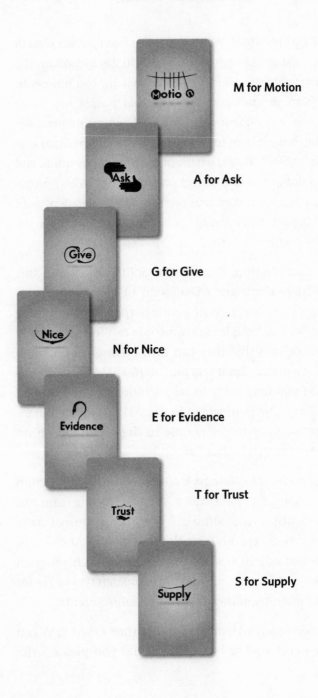

M for Motion

A for Ask

G for Give

N for Nice

E for Evidence

T for Trust

S for Supply

M STANDS FOR MOTION. We all remember from physics class in high school that an object in motion tends to stay in motion. The same is true when it comes to people making commitments. Research from psychologists suggests that people will move forward when they make **a series of small commitments.** Sales professionals have known for years that they want to obtain a series of small "yeses". That is what's called a yes momentum, and small commitments lead to larger commitments. When people make a commitment, they face pressure to be consistent with that commitment, and the more public the commitment is, the stronger the pressure they feel.

A recent example from Presidential politics illustrates this point. Whether you are a Democrat or a Republican (or something else) is not relevant for the purposes of identifying a best practice—although I know people can feel so strongly about their politics that they can turn themselves off when politics is discussed. But if you are interested in moving people forward you may want to take a moment and consider how one Party (the Democrats) in the 2012 Campaign managed to get so many more people to the voting booth on Election Day than the other Party.

As was reported in *The New York Times* following the election (and other sources) there was a sort of "dream team" of decision scientists (including a few of the authors I have mentioned) who were advising the Democrats. And one of their pieces of advice was that in their outreach program (door to door and on the phone) the campaign was to ask for small commitments, rather than large commitments.

When speaking with Democrat voters they asked "Do you have a pen and a piece of paper? Would you please write down the time you are going to vote on Election Day? And also, please write down how you are planning on getting to the voting booth."

Think about it—there are three small commitments there: get a pen, write down the appointed time, and name your ride.

Now let's consider why these small commitments were actually big things. What prevents many voters (particularly the elderly and the poor) from voting? It might be that if we don't have something written down in our calendar and if we haven't planned ahead for transportation, then we might be less likely to actually go vote.

It's up to you to consider not only what you want your prospects to do, but what are the obstacles that are stopping them from doing that. And research suggests that small commitments can actually move people forward faster than larger commitments.

A STANDS FOR ASK. When it comes to ask, remember my first law of selling: *the person who asks the questions controls the conversation.* And questions set the context for comparison, and decision making (and therefor successful selling) is really about context or comparison. In fact, much work in decision science supports this concept of perceptual contrast and what the scientists call "framing."

Psychologists in classes will use three buckets of water as an example of framing. Suppose the middle bucket is room temperature, the bucket on your right is almost boiling, and the bucket on the left is ice water. Put your right hand in the hot water, and you put your left hand in the cold water. Hold them there for a minute, and then immediately take both hands out and put them in the room-temperature water. How does the right hand that was in the hot water perceive the room temperature water? As cold. How does the left hand that was in the ice water perceive the room temperature water? As warm. Each hand perceives the middle bucket temperature differently, depending on what came first.

So the application here for us is that the questions we ask put people's hands in the buckets we want them to be in. For example, how does a 7 percent interest rate on a home mortgage sound? High or low? Well, it depends on what "bucket" of interest rate you were feeling before that. If you were consolidating a bunch of credit cards with total average interest rates over 17 percent, the 7 percent rate would feel low. But how would the 7 percent interest rate feel if your existing home loan was at 3.5 percent? Well, that same 7 percent would feel high.

It's up to you to put your customers' hands in the appropriate buckets and help them to understand and feel the correct context.

G STANDS FOR GIVE. Giving is a very powerful principle, especially in Western societies. In the United States, when someone gives you something, **you feel pressure to give something back** to them. This is what scientists call reciprocity. In our culture, we feel pressure to give back what we're given. That's because most of us were raised with a principle called the Golden Rule: Do unto others as you would have done unto you. If I bought you dinner and we're friends, you would feel pressure to buy me dinner the next time we were out.

So the key for us is this: what can you give a prospect? Giving compliments (as one example) can deliver huge payoffs. If, in the beginning of a phone call, you say something like, "You made a *really smart decision* to call in today," you're making small deposits in the reciprocity bank.

N STANDS FOR NICE. In my seminars, I ask attendees how many of them agree that they are more likely to buy from **people they like** than from people they don't like? Of course, nearly everyone says yes—we buy from people we like. As a follow-up, I ask how many people think business is just business. Of course, no one raises a hand. Scientists support the finding that we do business with people we like, and go even farther to say that people are influenced more by people they like than by people they dislike.

So the question for us then is what do scientists say are the triggers that can make us like someone?

I've summarized this research into what I call **the three Cs: Common, Compliment, Collaborate.** People like people who are like them, so the goal is to find things in common with your customers. Let them know what you have in common, because they're looking for reasons to like you. The second C is to compliment, because people like people who like them. So what can you find to pay an honest compliment on? It must be sincere, because people can see through phonies. The third C is collaborate, because people like people who are on their side. In an uncertain situation, the salesperson is basically putting an arm around us and saying, "Come with me. You're not alone."

The research into how people assess heights and distance (in other words how hard travelling a path might be) says that we will see distances as shorter and mountains as not so high when we are travelling with a friend. One example of this research was published in the October/November 2008 edition of *Scientific American MIND*.

Quite simply, we are more likely to be influenced by people we like—and to want them by our side when we are doing something hard.

E STANDS FOR EVIDENCE. The research suggests that when people are in situations of uncertainty, they look for evidence indicating they're about to make the right decision. What's McDonald's really communicating with its sign that says "Over 70 Billion Served"? It's saying two things: "It ain't great, but it probably won't kill you."

Seriously, scientists call this social proof. We're looking for evidence that a lot of other people like us are doing something, especially when we're in a situation of uncertainty. Remember that people don't gravitate toward the best choice; they move in the direction of the less risky choice.

What McDonald's slogan represents is certainty (read safety), and in times of economic uncertainty, people gravitate toward safe options. There is a flight to safety. This explains why the value of gold as an investment rises in time of economic uncertainty—because gold is perceived by investors as a safe option for their money. This might also explain—even more than low prices—why McDonald's has done so well in times of economic uncertainty (all-time record profits between 2009 and 2012). As I re-edit this book in May of 2013 both McDonald's recent profits and the price of gold have declined in direct correlation with the improvement in the economy. In other words, it could be that as people are feeling more safe those "standards of consistency" represented by McDonald's (as a place to eat) and gold (as an investment) are becoming less attractive.

Many folks may make the comment, "Wait a second, McDonald's is successful in a tight economy because of things like the Value Meal—it is the fact that they are the cheap option that makes them successful in tough times." But if that were the only reason (and McDonald's is successful for a lot of reasons) then wouldn't the OTHER fast food places all have shared in the growth that McDonald's experienced? The fact is they did not.

It is not a flight to "cheap" that explains the rise in the price of gold as an investment either—it is a flight to "safe".

So the question for us to ask is "Do the people we want to influence see us as safe or risky?"

T STANDS FOR TRUST. Research shows that people are more likely to be influenced by authority figures. People trust credible experts, and one of the clues people look for are trappings of authority like diplomas, awards, and certifications. When a person walks into a doctor's office, there's a diploma on the wall, which the patient can look at it before the doctor comes in. Doctors don't have diplomas on the wall because they forgot where they went to school, right? They're building a perception of their trustworthiness in advance.

What is your diploma? I share my diploma throughout my presentations, on my website—even at various places in the book you are reading:

9,000 CEOs and sales executives personally trained since 1992

350 workshops on better sales messaging in the last three years

22 years of identifying sales best practices

4.9 average rating on a 5-point scale from CEOs attending Talks

1 simple guide to help you get to yes faster

How can you and your team present *your* diploma?

S STANDS FOR SUPPLY. The psychological principle of scarcity says that limited supplies and deadlines motivate prospects to take action. A relatively short supply of something tells people that it's worthy of their attention. If something is limited in supply, it looks more valuable. Deadlines also relate to this scarcity or supply issue. We can guarantee that one of the busiest days at the post office in any town in the United States is April 15. That's because it's the deadline to file your taxes, and there's a risk of loss if we don't meet that deadline.

What is at risk for your clients? When you take into account the fact that research suggests that risk (and the threat of loss) can be up to twice as powerful a motivator as rewards, many of us would rewrite our messages. Because most marketing messages are *gain messages* not *loss messages*.

Several years ago an automobile manufacturer came up with a loss message that triggered Americans to visit their showrooms and consider buying their brand of cars during a time when Americans had stopped buying cars. It is considered one of the most effective messages in the history of selling cars. In fact, many times I will say to an audience, "I only have to share with you the first half of the message and you will be able finish it...

"If you lose your job, we will _____?" (and most of the audience will yell "we will take the car back.")

Go ahead and Google "The Hyundai Assurance Program" if you have time to look up the all the details on why "experts" believe the message was so successful.

The bottom line—it sold a TON of cars, and it had nothing to do with cars. It had to do with what was stopping people in America from buying cars—the **risk of losing their jobs.**

So take a moment and consider: first, what is at risk for your prospect or target; second, how can you make that risk clear to them; and third, how can you eliminate the risk?

How to Use These MAGNETS to Attract a Yes

When taken together, the seven principles outlined above go a long way to helping us understand why people say yes. And you can use them in an ethical and non-manipulative manner to attract a yes, which is why I refer to them as magnets.

Take out some blank paper, and write the word **MAGNETS**. For each letter, consider the following questions:

1.

M: How can I build *motion* in the beginning of my interaction? How can I get momentum? How can I get a series of yeses to build momentum?

2.

A: What are the questions I can *ask* to set the right context for my customers and control the conversation? How can I create the right framing (buckets of water)?

3.

G: What can I *give* the customer? Can I give him samples, information, or honest compliments to employ the reciprocity rule?

4.

N: Because people buy goods and services from people they like, what can I do to be *nice*? What do I have in common with them, how can I compliment them, and what actions can I show them that we're going to collaborate on?

5.

E: What *evidence* can I show them as social proof that others like what am offering? How many others have made this decision (and have survived)?

6.

T: Because people are looking to do business with people they *trust*, what can I do to establish that I am an authority? What can I show them about the firm's background and my own education and experience?

7.

S: How can I show the prospect (if appropriate) that there's a limited *supply* of what I offer or a deadline to take action? How can I honestly let the customer know what they stand to lose if they don't meet a certain dead-line with me?

Answer these questions before each sales presentation, and you'll be helping your prospects say yes to you.

There's another piece of the yes puzzle that I want to help you put together, that is, learning a language that every decision maker understands. You have to speak the same language as the decision maker that you are trying to get a yes from. What if there were three ancient words you could use that would guarantee that the decision maker is listening to you? There are three such words: **Alpha**, **Delta** and **Video**. And they are covered in the next lesson.

KEY QUESTION

HAVE YOU MADE IT ATTRACTIVE?

PERSONAL ACTION SUMMARY

Make a list of action items taken from your reading of this book:

LESSON 5

MAKE IT PERSONAL

Personal

This lesson contains three ancient words that are the critical elements you can use today to speak a language understood personally by every decision maker.

ALPHA   DELTA   VIDEO

Take a guess how many "sales", "marketing" and "influence" books there are available on Amazon.com today? A recent search showed me 349,363 books on the topic of sales, a whopping 548,151 on the topic of marketing, and an additional 65,245 on the topic of influence. And there are new books being published every week. Some of the information is new, but all of it will reaffirm three ancient truths: the first truth is that people care **about themselves** and their own survival; second, they **pay attention to changes** in their environment that affect them (see truth number 1); and third, that people believe the things that **they can see**.

I have several hundred "sales" books in my personal library—and no matter how recent the publication, every single one of them can have their major points summarized in three words that were known to the ancients: Alpha, Delta and Video.

I have a few dozen books that outline specific (and powerful) sales models, and again every single one of them can have their major points summarized in those same three words.

If you looked on my bookshelves you'd find at least fifty books worth reading on the topic of making presentations and influencing people—and, you guessed it, all can be summarized in three magic words.

ALPHA. The ancient Greeks used this word to represent the first letter of their alphabet and it still is used to indicate *"the first; beginning; something having the highest rank in a dominance hierarchy: the alpha female of an elephant pack."* The first thing (alpha) that anyone thinks about in any situation is themselves.

They are asking the question *"What's In It For Me?"* And I use the image of a radio station with the call sign "WIIFM" to represent this concept—every person, every place in the world is **listening to the signal from the station WIIFM.** How quickly can you tell your target the WIIFM? How quickly can you tell them that you understand their world—their problems?

The focus of your presentation should be on your audience—and letting them know as quickly as possible that you understand their world—what Keith Eades was calling "situational fluency" in his book *The New Solutions Selling* (with his focus on "Pain") is the same thing that David Ogilvy was talking about in 1983 in *Ogilvy on Advertising* when he said, "Do your homework."

DELTA. The ancients used this word to mean *"change; differ-ence,"* and it still is used today in mathematics as represented by the triangle symbol to indicate change. This symbol is really the heart of the One-Page Sales Coach model—because making a difference is what makes sales the most honourable of professions. How quickly can you tell your target what is going to change in their world?

Your ability to make a difference is your key to making a commission. All the books written on "positioning" and "differentiating" are at their core about *how you and your message is different from the "other"*. And keep in mind that the "other" is not always someone or something else—in fact in most cases the "other" is the "status quo". In other words you are competing against your target not doing anything. How will doing something with you be different than her not doing anything?

Mack Hanan's series of books under the titles of *Consultative Selling* throughout the 1980's were in depth guides to help you identify for your target the financial (and other) advantages that would accrue by them doing business with you. And advertisers from the *Mad Men* glory days right up to today have known the power of using "Before-and-After" illustrations and demonstrations. (see, *Ogilvy on Advertising*, page 77).

VIDEO. The word we say as "video" is actually an ancient word, in Latin dictionaries you will find the ancient word defined as *"to see, to perceive, to understand"*. We have all heard the phrase "A picture is worth a thousand words," and yet most presentations, most websites, most attempts to influence are muddied up with tons of words. How can you make your presentation more visual?

The power of visual processing is undeniable and well documented—and the decision sciences are just now explaining why. In my work in the early 1990's attempting to make performance numbers more visual for the sales people I was training I was impacted by the work of Yale professor Edward Tufte and his three beautiful books including *Visual Explanations* (all published in the early 1980's).

Influence professionals have known for decades the power of visual aides—whether it be J. Douglas Edwards teaching sales-people to use what he called "Visual Demonstration Closes" (these could include The Puppy Dog Close and The Ben Franklin Balance Sheet Close) back in the 1950's and 1960's to David Peoples' recommendations to the IBM Corporation in his 1992 work *Presentations Plus* to take out as many words as possible from their presentations and that "the best visual is the real thing—next best is a picture of it." (see Edwards' *Sales Closing Power* page 226, and Peoples' *Presentation Plus* page 249)

I know that these concepts are not new—my point is that they are in fact eternal and ancient truths that we all forget to apply. We can find examples throughout history of how folks have used these three words (Alpha, Delta and Video) as their guide to be more persuasive—and I guarantee you that if you keep them in mind when reading about "new findings" you will find these three concepts there.

A recent **Wall Street Journal** article documenting that advertisements for "Mansion" homes were more effective when they **showed pictures**, then when they don't (an example of the Video concept). Bill Clinton's first successful Presidential Campaign repeated the mantra "It's the Economy, stupid" to remind his team that that's **what the voters cared about** (Alpha, WIIFM). And these conceptual elements were present in the Hyundai Assurance Program message, "If you lose your job, we'll take the car back," (really all three: Alpha, Delta and Video). As we hear about and read these examples we say, in our own versions of the immortal words of Homer Simpson, "DOH!"

Because we may realize that we are **not** always applying these simple principles, are we?

A CEO once who asked me to help him get a "yes" from an executive at a major pharmaceutical company. At the beginning of our coaching session I asked, "Can you tell me what's in it for her—WHY she should say yes to you?"

"Because we can save her $9 million dollars in 60 days."

"Great—show me the presentation." And the CEO proceeded to fire up PowerPoint, and begin a 42 slide overview that he called his "Capability Deck." Can you take a guess what slide told the executive she was going to save $9 million in 60 days? *Slide 37.* He was planning on making her wait 36 slides before getting to the WIIFM! (The first ten slides were about HIM—by the eleventh slide the prospect would have been fighting to stay awake.)

And he's not alone—think about your last major attempt to influence and be honest: How long did it take you to get to the WIIFM?

From time to time we all forget the basics—every single one of us.

We forget that people care about what is in it for them (not us), they people care about what is different, and they want to see it.

For context, I will share that after twenty years of focusing on sales success and applied behavioral psychology, I believed I knew a little bit about selling. (That's when the trouble starts, when you start thinking you know a little bit about something, right?)

Well, in 2007, a friend of mine in California had published a top-selling book on Amazon.com. I was helping him set up a consulting business around this book. All of a sudden, he brought on a whole bunch of CEO clients in California, all at the same time. Meanwhile, another consultant-friend, down in Texas, started telling me about the many CEOs he was meeting.

Coincidence? I asked each of them, "Where are these clients and new contacts coming from? Where are you meeting these CEOs?"

They each told me that there is a "secret society" of CEOs that meets once a month.

"How did you guys get invited to this if it's a secret society?" I asked.

They said these CEOs meet in small groups once a month, and they bring in speakers. The group, of course, was Vistage International.

When I searched for Vistage on the Internet, it certainly was no secret. But how had I not known about this organization? I was amazed to find out that it had been in existence since the 1950s and was by this time the world's leading CEO membership organization.

So I made a call to Vistage headquarters in San Diego to learn more. The Vistage person I spoke with explained that their local groups were led by someone they called the chair (short for chairperson). They arranged for me to meet my local chair.

The questions that the chair asked me the day we met were profound. Never before had someone ask me such insightful questions. All of the questions were about me—and what I wanted to have happen in the future for myself, my family and my business.

"Do you do this every month with your members?" I asked.

"Yes," he said, "both as a group and then one-on-one."

"And you bring in speakers too?"

"Actually, we're the world's largest speakers group. Vistage has thousands of featured speakers, and I'll bring in eight of them this year."

"I want to join."

"I want you to join also, Dino. There's something else I want you to consider. You should think about becoming a Vistage chair."

Wow, what a compliment! I thought. But I had some reservations, and I reflected on them with myself. "My daughter's with me full time every other week. I'm dedicated to building my sales-training business. Let me just become a member first."

So my initial desire was to become a Vistage member—certainly to have access to this chair, to a wealth of CEOs, and to all the speakers. And the more I learned about Vistage, the more I started to feel that if Vistage still wanted me to consider becoming a chair, it was an incredible learning opportunity for me on many levels.

So I did attend and go through what Vistage calls "chair training," which was six days of sessions in San Diego. Then I could make an informed decision. Well, the six days turned out to be the most powerful six days of training and learning of my life.

Goodbye, Me and Hello, You

During the very full days of chair training, I met a number of speakers who would change my life because of the focus they had on making a difference. The speakers presented topics ranging from how to prepare and run meetings that could be as much fun for the attendees as the opening of Hollywood movies, to how to have "fierce conversations" that clarified for people the real issues they were facing and helped them move forward with their lives. But the underlying thread connecting all the speakers and the topics was this: *focus on the other, not on yourself.* Focus on making a difference for the other. Get yourself out of the way—so that you have the space for them and contributing to their world.

In other words, if I am seeking to work with you, and if I want to influence you, it's not about me—it's what I can do for you and with you to improve your condition that is important to you.

What the speakers were all illustrating is that people follow a process when they make decisions—and that process is about them. Now none of this was new to me—but it was in a way eye opening.

I had been asking some of the right questions in my work, but not all the right questions.

To recap, the first question is, *What if you could find out what top sales performers do?* (Having an understanding of sales best practices is important.) And the second question is, *What if you could find out why people say yes?* (Having a basic understanding of decision science is also important.)

And now the third question that guides my work:

How can you help people see what is in it for them so that they will say yes to you faster?

In much the same way that my earlier exposure to psychologists first turned me on to the world of behavioral psychology, these speakers were turning me on again to timeless principles that form the basis of decision making.

ALPHA means the first thing anyone thinks about in any situation is himself or herself. People focus on their own survival.

DELTA means difference, change. Before and after, big and small, loud and quiet are all examples. People pay attention to the Delta because any change in the environment might flag that you're in danger. People look to see differences; the greater the difference between two things, the easier it is for us to understand why to choose one thing over the other.

VIDEO means "to see". You can touch it, feel it, and it is easy to understand. People like things that are simple to understand. When it comes to survival, the eyes are critically important; our most important sense for survival is sight. Visual processing is important to your survival. Research suggests that information gets processed thirty times faster through the eyes than through the ears. So, the fastest way to get something into someone's head is through her eyes.

And it all struck me as not only common sense but consistent with all I had learned in my years of study of sales practices and behavioral psychology.

I eventually decided that the best way for me to contribute to the world was not as a Vistage chair (not yet at least, I'm saving that honor for later), but by combining my background and life study into Talks that could contribute to Vistage members the way the speakers that week resonated with me.

Take out another blank sheet of paper, and write the words Alpha, Delta and Video. For each letter of that word, consider the following questions:

1. ALPHA: Do I have a clear and quantifiable understanding of the client's *problems*? What questions would I need to ask to get my mind around his current situation? Can I say in one minute or less—"Here is what's in it for you in working with me." If I had the chance to say only one thing to him or to show one thing to him, what would that be?

 **ALPHA**

2. DELTA: How much will change in my client's world as a result of working with me; how big is the difference between the before and after? And how different is my solution from the other solutions available? The bigger the difference, the easier it will be for my customer to understand why they should say yes.

 **DELTA**

3. VIDEO: What can I show the client to make my message visible? Can I use physical objects? Can I show a video? Can I draw out the process on a map? Seeing is believing.

 **VIDEŌ**

When taken together, the three elements outlined above can help you to speak a language understood personally by every decision maker. And you can remember them as the three ancient words Alpha, Delta and Video which you can use to trigger a yes faster from anyone.

KEY QUESTION

ARE YOU MAKING IT PERSONAL?

MY PROBLEM
AT HAND

But I had a major problem as these speakers were presenting to us during that week of training. My emotions moved to panic. I actually put my head down on the table during one presentation and I said "Oh, *no*!"

The speaker looked at me with concern and said, "Dino, are you okay?"

"No, man," I said, "I am definitely not okay." What the speakers were teaching me was *triggering me* in a massive way. The lessons were a wake-up call. In just four weeks, I had an appointment with the famous CEO of a large manufacturing company. Getting an appointment with someone this important was a triumph, but each of the speakers in their own way had made me realize how woefully unprepared I was.

The CEO I was to meet is someone familiar to almost everyone in America because of his TV commercials. He wasn't just CEO; he was the inventor of the product.

One of my mentors, who did the CEO's media buying for his TV commercials, got me the appointment. The media buyer told the CEO that I could help him double his sales conversion rates.

These presentations made me realize that I knew nothing about the world of this CEO. After selling for twenty years, I was planning on flying to the CEOs office with at least one hundred PowerPoint slides I was ready to share. But guess who all those slides were about? That's right, me. This wasn't *you* messaging; it was *me* messaging.

Those slides should have been about the CEO's problems and solutions. I put my head down on the table, because I'd almost made a rookie mistake. Quickly I took corrective action. I came up with fifty questions and typed them up. Here are the first few:

1. What are all your marketing channels? And what is your response rate from each and your conversion rate from each?

2. What is your current sales training process?

3. What does your sales coaching look like?

4. What is the history of your company?

5. What is going on in your industry?

And on, and on, and on.

After I typed up the fifty questions, I went out on the balcony at lunch break and called Sam, the right-hand person of the CEO (their names have been changed for confidentiality).

"Sam, this is Dean Minuto. I have an appointment scheduled with your CEO."

"Yes," Sam said, "I see you here on Bob's calendar four weeks out. I knew I recognized your name. You were referred to us by someone we respect."

"Thank you," I said. "Sam, I was referred to you for one reason. I've been able to help companies like yours double their sales conversion rates. But for me to connect my knowledge with your world, there are some things I need to know that will help me save you and Bob time when I come down next month. So I'm e-mailing you a list of fifty questions, and with your permission, I'd like to fly down on Monday on my own dime. I want to spend three days on-site with you, doing research and learning about your current situation."

With Sam's permission, I flew down and spent three days at the company. When I asked these fifty questions, I found out a ton of useful information.

First, I found out they had a variety of advertising channels. They were getting a high amount of responses, but their conversion rate was only 2.7 percent. In One-Page Sales Coach terms, this is a dollar *problem* that belongs in the before box on the one-page sales coaching sheet.

This meant for every one hundred calls the company received from people wanting its product, they sold less than three. That sounded like a *problem* to me.

I also found out that products were tied up in the sales cycle for sometimes as long as three months. In other words, it was taking ninety days to complete a customer order. This was a *problem* I had data on now, and I also could put it in dollar form.

I found out that Bob's three largest competitors were under federal indictment for fraudulent practices. Sam told me that Bob hated the impression that people had about him and other manufacturers. He had started the business with his mom. He was a highly ethical man who invented a product to help people. The negative public perception was a deep personal pain (another *problem*).

Finally, Bob had gone outside the company for the first time for venture capital from a company in Chicago. The venture capitalists were extremely close to taking away his company from him. This was major pain.

My One-Page Sales Coach sheet started to look like this:

Problems *before*		Solutions *after*
Conversion rate at 2,7%	**Dollars**	Double conversion rate
Sales cycle up to 90 days	**Data**	Cut sales cycle in
VC's ready to take over the company	**Delta**	hall, double inventory turns
Damaged industry reputation		Investor satisfied Respected as ethical firm

Outcomes
great news

Do   Done   Demo

1.

2.

3.

Commitment
next steps

When I returned to my office, I plastered its walls with flipchart sheets outlining what I had learned at the meetings with the client organization. Everything I uncovered, I documented. I started getting Sam and his team on the phone and going deeper.

"Hey, Sam, what would it mean to your bottom line for every 1 percent that we're able to increase the conversion rate? How much in cash would that generate? What have you guys done so far? What haven't you tried? What's been the result?"

We talked about the sales cycle challenges. Sam started his team brainstorming ideas to free up that cycle after he and I created a map and began applying some methodology from my past work.

I spent the last two days before I went down to their office with a video camera set up in front of my desk. Over and over, I practiced what was going to be the first thirty seconds after Bob walked into the room.

From what I'd learned from the speakers in my Vistage training, I knew the CEO's decision was going to be made in the first one minute. That's how quickly people decide whether you are worth listening to.

Sam called me the day before I flew down. "Dean, I want to apologize before you come down."

"For what, Sam?" During the preparation, Sam and I had become friends.

"Our CEO has Attention Deficit Disorder bad; he may be the most ADD man on the planet. I just want you to be warned that he's going to push his chair back after about six minutes and leave the meeting. That's what happens."

That confirmed that I had to be prepared to grab his attention in the first minute or less.

The day of the meeting came. The CEO walked in, and I said, "Bob, I'm Dean Minuto. Thank you so much for having me here. *I'm here for three reasons, and only three, that matter to you.* And I've spent the last month studying with your Team why they're important to you.

"*Number one*, Bob, your conversion rate is stuck at 2.7 percent. Your team and I have brainstormed three specific ways to get that response rate to 4 percent within the next ninety days. That means 2.7 million in cash to your bottom line.

"*Number two*, Bob, right now your product can be tied up for ninety days in the sales process. We've identified ways to cut that in half this year; that would double your inventory turns, and with that improvement and the added cash, the investors in Chicago will be very happy.

"*And Bob, number three*, we'll do this in a way that treats your prospects with honor and respect, the way you and your mom always have.

"Bob, what if you could *accelerate* your sales cycles, *close* more business, and *trigger* clients in an honest and ethical way?"

And then I shut up.

That was the first one minute.

He leaned back, looked at me, and asked a one-word question, *"How?"*

And the hair stood up on the back of my neck, because When Bob asked "how" he was saying yes.

By asking "how?" he was saying, "Show it to me in 3D: what are you going to DO, who have you DONE it for, and give me a DEMO." Bob didn't spend just six minutes with me that day; he spent three hours.

I'd brought all my flipcharts with me. He had me paste them all over the conference-room walls. This was the result of the last four weeks of work I had done with his team. These flipcharts explained the **problems**, the **solutions**, the **outcomes** (accelerate, close, and trigger), and the commitment required for next steps.

The consulting deal with Bob and his company turned out to be a significant contract for me. More important, for their company *I made a difference*.

A few months later, every metric that we had projected would improve had, in fact, improved—and the company was on a much more firm financial setting.

Let me ask you this: Would I ever have gotten that deal if I had not gone down and talked with Sam? No. I'd been selling for twenty years, and I had forgotten to take a step back and document what was going on in their world and diagnose their **problems** and how their world could be different.

Now, the thing that's so impressive to me about this process is this: it reminds us what's so honorable about selling—selling is honorable because of the contribution (the change) we make to our customers world. This is summed up by the triangle between the Problems (Before) and the Solutions (After) boxes on the One-Page Sales Coach sheet.

When done right, selling is honorable because you are improving your customers' condition; you are making a difference in their world. As salespeople, we have both the privilege and the obligation to improve our customers' condition. By putting in that kind of time, I was able to identify how I could impact this CEO's world and improve his company's world for the better.

But let me tell you the amazing part. It isn't what happened the day I closed the deal. It's what happened the night before.

Remember that Sam had called me the day before I flew down? He had said, "Dino, I know you're flying a few hours to come meet with us. May I pick you up when you fly in, and we'll have dinner together?"

"That would be great, Sam," I said. "Thank you. I'm on the road a couple hundred days a year, and I hate having dinner by myself."

So Sam met me at the airport and took me out to dinner. I had a spark of intuition as the food was delivered and said, "Sam, I get the feeling you'd like to say grace."

"I would," he said. "Would that be okay?"

"Absolutely!" I said.

We bowed our heads, and I'll never forget what Sam said. *"Dear Lord, please help Dean close this deal tomorrow."*

My prospect was *praying* for me.

My prospect was praying that his boss would buy from me.

Take a moment and consider that fact.

I found this to be incredible—a prospect praying that a salesperson would close the deal with his boss. Why was Sam praying for me? What did I represent to him?

Safety, trust, and *outcomes* that represented a better world. That was what my preparation had earned. Sam knew how hard I was preparing for this one deal—and *he and I* had prepared for four weeks together. Many times clients can benefit from us taking the time to assist them in getting a true handle on the *problems* that the organization, and their boss, are experiencing. He and I had worked together on understanding it and creating a plan to improve it.

It has been my experience that many people don't take this kind of time to understand the world of the person they want a yes from. Most sales professionals and organizations don't spend even four minutes in preparation. Instead, they wing it. They have no process like the One-Page Sales Coach to organize their thoughts.

Sam and his team now had a much better sense of the problems they were facing—and he knew he needed help. I was that help.

In the business world, we've come to the conclusion that you're either a closer—you know how to sell—or you don't. We don't train; we don't practice.

Now that you've read this far in this book, there is no excuse for not preparing. All you need to start is a blank sheet of paper and a pen to prepare for a sales presentation. To review, whether you have four weeks or four minutes, prepare for the presentation with the following steps:

1. PROBLEMS. Start with the *before* box to understand where the client is right now. Ask questions to uncover the prospect's real situation. Find out what she has tried before and what is preventing her from getting what she wants.

2. SOLUTIONS. Proceed to the *after* box of the grid. Ask questions to understand the prospect's goals, wants, and desires.

3. OUTCOMES. Move down to the *great* news box. This is when you have earned the right to ask questions like, "Based on what you've shared, if I could show you a way to achieve the benefits you want would that be of value to you?" It's important for the customer that you do this with confidence.

4. COMMITMENT. A presentation ends by proceeding to the *next steps* box. This is when you summarize and gain a clear commitment for the next step in the process.

What's Next

After preparation comes presentation. That means a return to the first law of selling: ***questions control the conversation***. Next comes a lesson on the importance and application of this first law.

PERSONAL ACTION SUMMARY

Make a list of action items taken from your reading of this book:

LESSON 6

MAKE IT HAPPEN

Happen

In this lesson, I'll discuss the importance of knowing specifically what you want the client to do or say—the result you want to achieve—and how asking questions allows you to control the flow of client conversations.

In the One-Page Sales Coach process, the salesperson's goal is to reach the fourth box: Commitment. There's a path to getting to that point, and following that path requires that the salesperson take control of the conversation by asking the right questions.

To illustrate this point (and a few sales best practices), I use a fun card trick during my presentations. The card trick goes something like this.

<u>DEAN:</u>   Who plays cards? Please raise your hand if you play cards. I need two volunteers. (Pat and Chris raise their hands, indicating that they play cards),

Great. Pat, come up here for a moment to the front of the room.

Best Practice - Prequalify: I pick folks who can help me with my "trick" because they play cards—make sure you prequalify who you're dealing with.

DEAN:
(whispers)
Pat, thank you. Now, come behind the flipchart with me where nobody in the room can see you. (I have turned the flipchart stand backward so the audience can't see it.) I'd like you to pick a card, any card from the deck. And please, I would like you to draw it on the flip-chart. You can show it to me as you draw it. (Pat draws the four of diamonds in red marker on the flipchart and shows only Dean.)

Best Practice - Begin with the End in Mind: I now have my goal, the four of diamonds.

DEAN:
Thank you, Pat. Now, Chris, how many cards are in the typical deck?

CHRIS:
Uhhh, let me think (he's nervous because he's in front of a large group). Ummm, forty-nine! (The audience groans because he gave a wrong answer, but here comes a best practice.)

DEAN:
Great, forty-nine cards. Let's go with that. Now among the forty-nine cards there are two colors, red and black. Isn't that correct?

Best Practice - Never Argue with a client about stuff that's irrelevant to getting you to your goal. Forty-nine cards or fifty-two cards—who cares?

CHRIS: Correct.

DEAN: Chris, between red and black, which do you prefer?

CHRIS: Red.

DEAN: The red ones. Excellent. We're going to talk about the red cards for now. Fair enough?

CHRIS: Yes.

DEAN: Now, among the reds, there are two kinds of suits. There's diamonds and hearts, correct?

CHRIS: Correct.

DEAN: Between diamonds and hearts, which do you prefer?

CHRIS: Hearts.

DEAN: We're going to go ahead and set the hearts aside— over here in the parking lot (I motion off to my right side, like I'm taking something off the table). We're going to come back to them in a moment. Let's go ahead and talk about the diamonds for now. Fair enough?

CHRIS: Sure.

Best Practice - Build a Parking Lot. Move everything that takes you away from your goal to the parking lot to discuss at another time.

DEAN: Now, among the diamonds there are two kinds of cards. There are face cards and number cards, correct?

CHRIS: Correct.

DEAN: Between face cards and number cards, which do you prefer?

CHRIS: Face cards.

DEAN: Face cards. Okay. We're going to set those over here—in the parking lot again—with the hearts. We're going to come back to them in one moment. Let's go ahead and talk about the number cards within the diamonds. Fair enough?

CHRIS: Yes.

DEAN: Now, among the numbers within the diamonds, you've got odd numbers and even numbers, correct?

CHRIS: Correct.

DEAN: Between odd and even, which do you prefer?

CHRIS: Even.

DEAN: Even. Let's go ahead and talk about the even numbers among the diamonds. Fair enough?

CHRIS: Okay.

DEAN: Now, among the diamonds and these even numbers, what would be the second lowest even number among the diamonds?

CHRIS: Four.

DEAN: Four of diamonds. That's interesting. Let's see what card Pat selected. (Here I turn the flipchart around so that the room can now see that Chris "picked" the hidden card.) Why, it's the four of diamonds! How did you do that, Chris?

Start With the End in Mind and Control the Conversation

There's a really important concept and a lot of little sales best practices all wrapped up in this card trick example. In fact, if I were to share with a new salesperson the top five best practices in selling, the card trick illustrates them all.

The number-one best practice comes from Stephen Covey, author of *The Seven Habits of Highly Effective People:* "Start with the end in mind."

There's only one thing I needed to know before I started asking Chris questions. I needed to know what card was selected, which in this example was the four of diamonds. Many salespeople don't have an end in mind when they walk in to speak to a client. But if they don't have a goal, they end up floating all over the place.

I always ask the crowd, "Who picked the card?"

They usually yell back, "You did!"

"Nope, I did not." Then I ask the person who volunteered, the one who drew the card. "Pat, who picked the card?"

And the volunteer says, "When I walked up there, Dean asked *me* to pick the card—the four of diamonds was *my* choice."

I want to point out that, in selling, *we* usually don't get to "pick the card"; our boss or our firm is picking the card (the product) we're selling.

The key is the next question I ask the room, "Who was in control of the conversation—me or Chris?"

Always the answer is, "*You* were in control, because you were asking the questions."

Remember best practice number two: pre-qualification. What was the question I asked the room before I picked Pat to come up and work with me? "How many of you play cards?" So I prequalified. Chris and Pat raised their hands, so I had my two guys to play.

Then I brought Pat up, and I had him pick the card. I said, "Pick any card in the deck. Pick red or black." And he picked red. I said, "Draw it up there on the flipchart."

Once he had picked that card, I was unstoppable in getting someone to my card. But here's the key: you have to know the card you want to get to before you start.

Now, let me just stop here for a second. I want to reiterate this because it's key: Most salespeople don't know the card they want to get to in any given sales call. And most CEOs and sales executives don't know the card they want to get to in a meeting.

What I mean is this: What is the actual result you want to end up with at the end of the meeting? What's the commitment you want to end up with? What do you want the customer doing, saying, asking for from you, or providing to you? What are the next steps?

Once I know four of diamonds, I'm unstoppable if my questioning technique is sound. I've never been stopped from getting to the card I want to get to. Best practice number three is to have your questions framed so you stay in control.

I've coached thousands of CEOs and sales executives, and I can tell you that the minute a salesperson or a CEO loses control of a presentation is the minute a customer starts asking the questions and directing the flow of the conversation.

Now we get to best practice number four, which is to ignore the irrelevant. Remember when Chris said there were forty-nine cards in the deck?

When I coach salespeople, I hear them arguing with customers about stuff that's irrelevant, because they don't know where they're trying to get to. They want to prove that they're smarter than the customer. You being smarter than the customer is irrelevant. Is "forty-nine" or "fifty-two" going to get me to my four of diamonds any quicker? Nope.

So we ignore the irrelevant—especially if correcting our customer in front of a group of people is going to embarrass them.

Then I started asking questions. Between red and black, which did he prefer? Red. "Among the red, you've got two suits—hearts and diamonds." What did I want him to pick? Diamonds. What did he pick? Hearts. What did I do then? I had him agree to set the hearts aside.

This is best practice number five, which is creating a "parking lot." If an issue is brought up that just might take you to a place you can't go, you say, "You know what? I'm going to put that over here, in the parking lot in my notepad, because we're going to come back to it and give it the time it deserves. Let's start by talking about [the path you want to go on]. Is that okay with you?"

Remember that in my card trick example I asked him, "Do you want diamonds or hearts?"

He said, "Hearts."

I said, "Okay. We're going to talk about diamonds. Fair enough?" And what did he say?

He said okay. Why did he say okay? Who was in control? I was. That's because I was asking the questions and because I had a goal in mind.

The four boxes of the One-Page Sales Coach make up the card—getting the four boxes filled is like getting to the four of diamonds in the example above. Your goal is to be prepared and to be able to ask enough questions so that the client helps you fill the four boxes.

Now, this card trick example can strike some people as kind of manipulative. Please see past that to the message, because the card trick is used as a way to illustrate some important sales best practices.

If you're responsible for training a group of salespeople, and you believe they could benefit from a refresher in the above best practices, consider using the card trick yourself.

By the way, it's not as easy as it sounds! So practice it first.

Here are five questions you might ask of yourself and your team to implement the five best practices discussed in this lesson:

1. Do you have a **clear goal** in mind for the end of this meeting? In other words, "What is *the* card you're trying to get to?"

2. Have you **prequalified** the prospects involved? Are you certain you're meeting with the right people?

3. Do you have your **questions** laid out so that you can stay in control? What questions might the prospect ask to take you off your path, and are you prepared for each so that you can maintain control?

4. Can you **ignore** the irrelevant? In other words, can you avoid arguing with the prospect about stuff that doesn't matter?

5. Have you practiced building a **parking lot** to direct topics that might take you off your path, so that you can answer them more fully and appropriately later?

KEY QUESTION

WHAT DO YOU WANT TO HAPPEN?

A SPEECH WITH THE END IN MIND

One year, a number of years ago, I had an assignment from a nationally known retailer to visit a half dozen of their more than twenty call centers around the country. Then they wanted me to give a summary presentation to all their managers and teach them about my sales coaching model. They brought all their managers together for my event, so there were hundreds of people in attendance at the talk in Orlando. I'll never forget when John, the executive who ran the group, said, "Dino, you'd better be worth the money I've spent on this event."

"What do you mean?" I asked.

"Look, I've paid you a lot of money, and this is a tough audience."

"John, if I don't get a standing ovation, I'll give you your money back." I was pretty arrogant at the time.

"Dino, did you really just say that? Did you really just say if you don't get a standing ovation, you'll return your fee?"

"That's right. That's how confident I am."

"Listen, my people have never given a standing ovation."

"That's fine. John. I'm here to make a difference, and I'm confident that, after visiting the centers and customizing my message to your team, I will."

The session I delivered that day lasted more than four hours. I went through my whole coaching model, and I knew that the audience was still with me. At the end I said, "Guys, I'd like everyone to stand up. It's time to stretch. I've got one final slide to share with you, but before that, let's all get a little stretch in."

As everyone was standing and stretching out, I put an image on the screen of a mountain with a climber who's almost to the top. You can see him climbing the mountain, and in the background there's a quote. PowerPoint builds it up word by word, and I start reading the quote: "I'd like to end this session with my favorite quote from Henry David Thoreau. Thoreau said if a person [Thoreau said "A man." It was the 1800s after all] advances *confidently* in the direction of their dreams and *endeavors* to live the life they imagined, they will meet with a success *unexpected* in common hours."

I paused to let the power of Thoreau's words hit their mark. And then I said, "That's what I wish for this team. *A success unexpected in common hours*. You are such a terrific group of people. You have done so much and achieved so much in this year. I have all the faith in the world that you as a team are going to achieve a success unexpected in common hours in the year ahead. And I am so honored to have been here today, to contribute in some small way to your continued success, thank you very much."

Then I started clapping for them, and the entire audience started clapping with me. **And then I bowed.**

There it was: my standing ovation. As I continued to bow and said thank you to the group, I pointed at John and winked.

John sprang from his seat and said, "Wait a second. Wait!" He jumped out of his chair, came on stage, took the microphone from me, and said, "I have to stop you. I have to stop this. People, I want you to understand what just happened. I'm sitting there and I'm observing my team give this man a standing ovation. I've never seen this before, and then I realized what happened. He had you all stand up; already he's halfway to a standing ovation. Then he reads you this inspiring Henry David Thoreau quote, says it's about you. He starts clapping for you, and of course you joined him. And then he *bows*? This is the first man I've ever seen give himself a standing ovation!"

There was a lot of laughter that day. Presenting, like selling—heck, like *everything in life*—is all about knowing the results you want to achieve and then taking the necessary steps to make them happen.

Keep thinking about the fourth box: Commitment and Next Steps. Ask yourself. "What is the next step I want the customer to take?" What do you want them asking for? What do you want them requesting? What do you want them scheduling? Everything you do with the One-Page Sales Coach process should be about getting to that end.

PERSONAL ACTION SUMMARY

Make a list of action items taken from your reading of this book:

_____

_____

_____

_____

_____

_____

_____

_____

_____

_____

_____

_____

_____

_____

_____

_____

_____

_____

_____

_____

_____

A Final Thought

Bobbie Carlyle has created some of the most compelling figurative sculptures in the world today, works that cause viewers to look into themselves, because the sculptures can convey several layers of meaning. Indeed, her work carries a strong psychological appeal and deals with the full spectrum of life's struggles and triumphs.

I first saw one of her most famous works, *Self Made Man*, more than a decade ago—and it just blew me away. Even today that work resonates with me as one of the most powerful visuals I have ever seen. *Self Made Man* is a sculpture of a man using a hammer and chisel to carve himself out of stone; he is figuratively carving his character and carving his future.

If you type "Bobbie Carlyle Self Made Man" into an Internet search engine, you'll see an image of the statue (or go to her website at www.bobbiecarlylesculpture.com).

Because this sculpture is a personal favorite, I end all of my introductory sessions with a reference to it—and tell everyone to look up Bobbie's work. What we're looking at is a man actually carving himself out of a block of granite.

Incidentally, Bobbie has a follow-up piece called *Self Made Woman*. *Self Made Woman* is Bobbie's vision of a woman creating herself from pliable yet strong clay, making her life and future to the smallest detail.

When I first saw *Self Made Man*, I was so taken with it I had to reach out and introduce myself to Bobbie and tell her how much the piece resonated with me.

There's an ancient phrase, "They themselves are makers of themselves." This is a theme found in every ancient book of wisdom, from the writings of the Stoics to the *Bible*. And as I've shared with you in this book, it's the theme of modern scientific study in expectancy theory; we bring into our reality the things we think about. And what we believe, with confidence, we can make our reality.

The man of the sculpture has a vision of what he wants to create in his life for himself, and he's actually carving himself out of stone. As Bobbie would tell you, if you look closely at the statue, he actually has the scars to prove it.

I was able to save up and buy an almost three-foot bronze of *Self Made Man*, which is in the foyer of my house. I also bought a version of the sculpture for my inspiration to make a difference, my father.

I show CEOs and salespeople this statue, because I really believe that when it comes to success in selling, this is what it means to be a sales professional. We create the outcomes we want for our customers. Our intent is to improve their condition and make a difference. Many folks go into sales because they want to build the kind of income and the kind of career they want; the most successful are those who focus on making a difference in the lives of others.

To me, Bobbie's statue is the most powerful visual metaphor in the world. I end my sessions by saying, "If you look at this statue, you see he's holding a hammer and he's holding a chisel. He's using these tools to carve himself out of a block of granite. My goal is to contribute to you. My goal is to help the teams, CEOs, and individual sales executives that I work with to carve out the outcomes they want. I view the models I've put together as tools—like that hammer, like that chisel—to help them make themselves, their business and the outcomes they want for their customers."

I encourage you to take the One-Page Sales Coach as a tool and a process into your world and use it to *make a difference* in your customer's world.

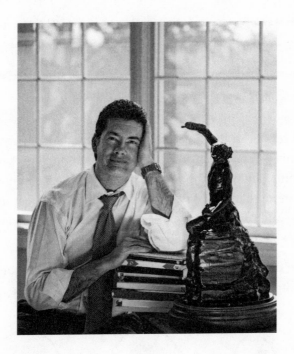

ABOUT THE AUTHOR

Dean Minuto helps professionals get to "yes" faster and more often from the people they are trying to influence. Dean teaches massively distilled summary courses to CEOs within the world's leading CEO membership organizations and to industry groups across the United States.

9,000 CEOs and sales executives personally trained since 1992

350 workshops on better sales messaging in the last three years

22 years of identifying sales best practices

4.9 average rating on a 5-point scale from CEOs attending Talks

1 simple guide to help you get to yes faster

Dean resides in the horse country of Chester County, Pennsylvania—just outside of Philadelphia— although his keynote, coaching, and workshop delivery schedule keeps him on the road more than 150 days a year. Dean holds degrees in marketing and finance, and earned a professional certification in behavioral psychology with Dr. Robert Cialdini.

Please email Dean@OnePageSalesCoach.com with questions regarding Coaching or delivery of a Talk for your group.

KEYNOTES **WORKSHOPS** **COACHING**

You will find access to his 30-second tip newsletters (that's how long they take to read) and other tools at **www.OnePageSalesCoach.com**

This book is available at special quantity discounts to use as premiums and sales promotions, or for use in corporate training programs.

Dean's new book, **YESCALATE: Get to YES Faster** will be available in 2014 - you can find more information at **www.yescalate.com** as well as an excerpt in the back of this book.

The following pages are graphics of the main tools you read about in The One-Page Sales Coach and are provided for your notes.

TOOL 1: The One-Page Sales Coach

TOOL 2: The Seven MAGNETS Strategies

TOOL 3: The Three Words

BONUS TOOL 4: The Wheel Alignment sample from Dean's new book YESCALATE: Get to YES Faster.

TOOL NUMBER 1:
The One-Page Sales Coach

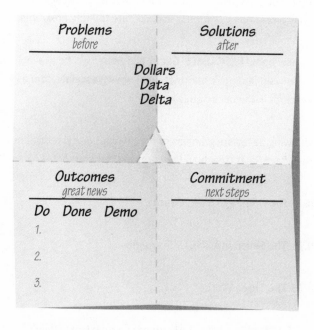

One-Page Sales Coach
Notes

TOOL NUMBER 2:
The MAGNETS

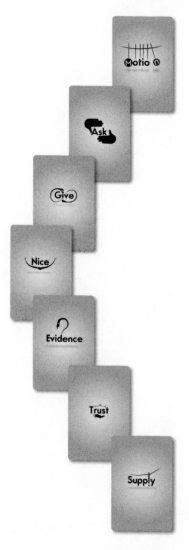

The following are trademarks of Teligent Corporation and Dean Minuto:
The MAGNETS™, and the Seven Magnets icons™
©2001 – 2013 Teligent Corporation and Dean Minuto

The MAGNETS
Notes

TOOL NUMBER 3:
THE THREE WORDS

 **ALPHA**

 **DELTA**

 **VIDEO**

The Three Words
Notes

BONUS TOOL:
The Wheel Alignment

PERSONAL

PROFESSIONAL

The Wheel Alignment™ Teligent Corporation and Dean Minuto
©2001 – 2013, Teligent Corporation and Dean Minuto
YESCALATE™ and GET TO YES FASTER™ Registration Pending

Excerpt from Dean's second book: YESCALATE

For folks who have attended my *YESCALATE* talk this tool will be familiar already—it is a powerful way to help sales professionals to do three things:

1) *Change the "paradigm" about themselves and training.* (We want them thinking of themselves as high performance machines.)

2) *Make Key Performance Indicators visual.* (And this is a visual metaphor that everyone "gets" very quickly.)

3) *Take ownership of their improvement.* (People "buy in" to those things they play a part in developing.)

You will note there are 5 spokes on each wheel to the left—indicating the five critical success areas to a sales professional in their PERSONAL and PROFESSIONAL life. And each of those spokes has a rating (from 0 to 5).

Take a moment and with a pen give yourself a rating on each spoke by circling a number from 0 to 5—and then "connect the dots" on each wheel.

How well would a car drive if its front tires looked like the ones you just drew? Are you in alignment today?

Next to each wheel set a few goals for yourself to get your wheels aligned—it's one of the key concepts from *YESCALATE* and will help you "Get to YES Faster."

Learn more at **www.yescalate.com** where you will also find access to Dean's email tip newsletter.

PERSONAL ACTION SUMMARY

Make a list of action items taken from your reading of this book:

Author's note on Trademarks

There are a number of trademarks mentioned in this book including but not limited to: *Amazon.com, Morton's, D&B, McDonald's, The Wall St. Journal, Vistage, Volvo, GE, Sears, H&R Block, Advanta, The New York Times, Hyundai* and *Google*. Each of these trademarks is owned by their respective owners. I mention the trademarks for instructional purposes only and not to imply a relationship to the owners of these marks or to create a likelihood of confusion as to the source, sponsorship, affiliation, or endorsement of the listed trademarks or goods associated with those trademarks.